CHRISTIAN MORGENSTERN'S
GALGENLIEDER

cHRISTIAN MORGENSTERN'S GALGENLIEDER

A SELECTION

Translated, with an Introduction, by MAX KNIGHT

UNIVERSITY OF CALIFORNIA PRESS

1963 BERKELEY AND LOS ANGELES

University of California Press
    Berkeley and Los Angeles, California
Cambridge University Press
    London, England
© 1963 by Max E. Knight

    Alle Galgenlieder, published in German by Verlag Bruno Cassirer, Berlin, 1933

Library of Congress Catalog Card Number: 63-15470

Designed by Jane Hart

Printed in the United States of America

Dem Mädchen der Bergwiese

CONTENTS

Christian's Zoo

Fairyland

Palmstroem and Korf

"Lorsqu'elles sont belles elles ne sont pas fidèles,
et lorsqu'elles sont fidèles, elles ne sont pas belles."
(INTRODUCTION, THOMAS MANN,
Doctor Faustus, AMERICAN EDITION)

"Translating from one language into another is like
gazing at a Flemish tapestry with the wrong side out."
(SAMUEL PUTNAM, *The Ingenious Gentleman Don Quixote,*
QUOTING CERVANTES)

"He who makes a literal translation of a verse of
Scripture is a liar, and he who adds to it a blasphemer."
(JEHUDA BEN ILAI, CITED BY P. A. HILTY
IN NOVALIS' *Henry of Ofterdingen*)

INTRODUCING
CHRISTIAN MORGENSTERN

When the Galgenlieder were first published in Ger-
many in March, 1905, many readers and critics were
puzzled, and the publisher received unflattering
mail. But others chuckled, and critic Julius Bab
wrote in the first review on May 20 of that year: "I
am sorry for those who do not sense the magnificent
subtle humor of the heart behind these crazy verse
fancies." [1] Between these two groups there has been
little middle ground.

Morgenstern scribbled the first of his capricious,
whimsical Galgenlieder in his twenties, when, as he
tells the story, on the occasion of a carefree outing
to Werder near Potsdam with some of his friends,
they passed a height locally known as Gallows Hill.[2]

---

[1] "Leid tut mir jeder, der bei diesem tollen Versspuk
nicht spürt, wie prachtvoll seelische Heiterkeit sich hier
birgt." Michael Bauer, *Christian Morgensterns Leben und
Werk* (2d ed.; München: R. Piper-Verlag, 1937), p. 158.
[2] Christian Morgenstern, *Ueber die Galgenlieder* (Ber-
lin: Cassirer-Verlag, 1921), pp. 10, 13.

1

In a mood of horseplay, they founded a "Club of the Gallows Gang," and Morgenstern wrote some grotesque verses, never meant for publication, that afterward were set to music by one of the group. They later continued their skylarking and met in a room equipped with the abstruse paraphernalia of a fraternity devoted to the cult of the gallows—a dark light from which dangled a crimson "life thread" (a noose?), a table covered with a black cloth, an hour glass, a rusty "blood-spattered" sword, a burning candle, phosphorescent symbols.

The members bestowed upon themselves gruesome-grotesque names [3] and peopled the gallows' world of Morgenstern's verses with weird humans and fabulous animals. The confines of this world were soon extended beyond the narrow limits of the Gallows Hill to include the vast landscape of Morgenstern's romantic world. Within a short time the Galgenlieder caught the popular fancy, found their way onto the stage of Ernst von Wolzogen's literary cabaret, and were eventually published by reckless Bruno Cassirer in Berlin, after three other publishers—Bondi, Schuster und Löffler, Albert Langen—had rejected them: his poems did not fit the traditional blasé cynical or satirical-ironical-tired humor pattern of the *Fliegende Blätter* or *Simplizissimus*.[4]

Morgenstern lived to see fourteen editions. By 1929, 100,000 copies of the original slender volume had been sold. An expanded volume that included later verses was published under the name of *Alle*

[3] Verreckerle, Bruder Schuhu, Unselm, Spinna, Stummer Hannes, Veitstanz, Gurgeljochem; Morgenstern was Rabenaas. (From the introduction of *Alle Galgenlieder*).

[4] Friedrich Hiebel, *Christian Morgenstern* (Bern: Francke-Verlag, 1957), p. 164.

Galgenlieder in 1932 and sold 290,000 copies by 1937. Later figures have not been made public. Some poems were set to music and some inspired paintings by Paul Klee ("Glockentönin BIM," "Das einsame Knie"). Most translations in the present volume are from *Alle Galgenlieder;* "The Snail's Monologue" and "Bohemian Carnival" are from *Egon und Emilie.* The grouping into sections was made by the translator.

The focus of the Galgenlieder world is Gallows Hill. The hill may not be so dramatic as Goethe's Blocksberg, but it is as alive. It is here that the moonsheep, the nightwindhound, and the fingoor roam. The Funnel, the Lone Knee, the Wentall travel the byways surrounding the hill; the inventive Korf, the sensitive aesthete Palmstroem, and the retiring Palma Kunkel live in the town that lies in the valley below it; the German A-and-Z moon shines cheerfully upon the corpses dangling from the gallows.

A large number of Morgenstern's Galgenlieder [5] are based on visual pictures that fascinated him. He "saw" things like a painter—his father and both grandfathers, Josef Schertel and Christian E. B. Morgenstern whose work can be seen in German art galleries, were all landscape artists of the romantic school. Thus Christian Morgenstern is an heir of the romanticists, just as he is a precursor of the surrealists. When he sees, presumably in a zoo, a

[5] B. Q. Morgan ("The Superior Nonsense of Christian Morgenstern," *Books Abroad,* summer, 1938, pp. 288 ff.) "categorizes" Morgenstern's poems into the following groups: "sheer nonsense, rhyme nonsense, punning fancies, sound effects, printed shapes, satires, philosophic concepts, sensible ideas grotesquely presented, bizarre ideas, and superior nonsense."

kangaroo watching a frightened sparrow on a fence post, this situation,[6] and nothing more, is the poem. Nothing "happens." The poem could end after the first two lines: "Behind the fence, the kangaroo/ has on a sparrow cast his view." But these lines are very suitable for book illustration, stick in the mind, and we are likely to remember them when we visit a zoo and see a chance sparrow there. The hen in the railroad station and the rocking chair on the terrace are also "visual verse." Morgenstern's grotesque animal world is a true heritage from his romantic-artist forebears; his creatures inhabit the German fairy-tale forest. The Nosobame is a cousin of Böcklin's unicorn in "Schweigen im Walde."

Another group of his verses deals with mechanical "inventions." Korf invents a clock that goes forward and backward at the same time, and Palmstroem has one that adjusts itself to the owner's wish to have time go faster or slower—"a clock with a heart." Sometimes Morgenstern enjoys carrying one of these inventive ideas to its absurd extreme, as in "Bohemian Carnival"; at other times he just tosses out a thought and leaves it to cling like a bur to the mind of the reader.

Above all, however, the Galgenlieder are preoccupied with words, with sounds, and with the foibles of the German language. Most of the "word" poems are pure mirthful impertinence, reflections of the good-natured sophistication of high-school students, and focus on the traps, pitfalls, and curiosities of the language. Morgenstern was fascinated by phonetics and linguistics: He remembered the playful word formations of his childhood, investigated the artificial international language of Volapük, studied Horace and Homer in the original, and translated

[6] *Ueber die Galgenlieder*, p. 12.

4

Ibsen, Strindberg, and Björnson. As a high-school student he "invented" a language. In this language —his own Volapük—the "Great Lalulā" is written, which, he once explained, is "not an expression of nonsense," but a "phonetic rhapsody," the mirror of "a highly personal, youthful *Uebermut*, which enjoys combinations that are very common among children, but are regarded as bizarre when encountered among adults." [7] If the kangaroo group of poems is based on the eye, the Lalulā group ("The Does' Prayer," "Problem," "Fish's Night Song," "Snail") is based on the ear. Morgenstern delightfully suggested additional punctuation marks [8] (while evidently considering semicolons as superfluous in "In the Land of Punctuation") and wrote a poem ("Der neue Vokal") about a newly invented vowel, "which the inventor will not pronounce, because it is not yet patented." Morgenstern plays with words as a child plays with blocks, piling them up, rearranging them, knocking them down. All his life he preserved the child's vision: to see words (and things) as though he had never seen them before; and he played with them as imaginatively as a child. Paraphrasing Nietzsche's "In any true man hides a child who wants to play," Morgenstern dedicated the Galgenlieder to "the child in man."

Some verbal quibbles had a special appeal for Morgenstern, because they enabled him to upset the "Philistine's" smug feeling of security. "To me," he said, "the term middle-class connotes a safe, comfortable, middle-of-the-road policy. Above all, our language is 'middle class,' in the middle of our road.

[7] *Ibid.*, p. 11.
[8] Christian Morgenstern, *Stufen* (München: R. Piper-Verlag, 1922), p. 100.

To drive it to one side or the other, or even off the road, is the noblest task of the future." [9] Applying himself to this noble task, Morgenstern took literally such untranslatable idioms as "die Flinte ins Korn werfen" and used them as subjects for his verses. Had he been an American he probably would have been tempted by the original flavor of "by the skin of one's teeth," "greased lightning," "dragging a red herring," or similar metaphors. He is likely to have chuckled over the wentletrap shell (the shift of the association from Treppe to trap), and would perhaps have allowed himself some low-brow capers about an icicle envying a bicycle, a Hebrew chiding a Shebrew, an out-law wishing to be an in-law, or an egret missing his egress (and turning back as regret) —about any linguistic caprice or coincidence. "Often I am struck in amazement about a word: I suddenly realize that the complete arbitrariness of our language is but a part of the arbitrariness of our world in general." [10]

Morgenstern felt that people use their familiar language unthinkingly, mouthing what they had heard before. "Most people do not talk—they quote. One feels tempted to put quotation marks around almost everything they say, because they have not themselves created the form of what they say, but merely followed habit." [11]

"His wit plays—and with how clear a flame!— round the idiocy of our faith in words, which possibly convey no ideas at all, or, if they do, problematic ideas." [12] Morgenstern said about man's unthinking use of language: "I don't want to see man shipwrecked, but he should be conscious of the fact

[9] *Ibid.*, p. 101.
[10] *Ibid.*, p. 100.
[11] *Ibid.*, p. 102.
[12] Jethro Bithell, *Modern German Literature* (London: Methuen, 1939).

6

that he's sailing on the high seas." [13] But not all Galgenlieder had such "ulterior motives." Some were undoubtedly sparked simply by rhymes and some by those lucky verbal accidents which he loved to exploit and which resulted in a humor sui generis. The public and the critics repeatedly insisted on reading all kinds of interpretations even into that group of Galgenlieder that were purely fun. Morgenstern mildly chided these pedants in his mock explanations by "Dr. Jeremias Müller" printed in *Ueber die Galgenlieder,* a "commentary" to the Galgenlieder.

As though Morgenstern had anticipated contrived attempts to read more into his fancies than he had put into them, he made clear in his "Aesthetic Weasel" that the rhyme, and no "deeper meaning," caused him to write at least this particular jingle. The "Wiesel" sitting on a "Kiesel" in "Bachgeriesel" can justifiably be translated as a ferret nibbling a carrot in a garret, a mink sipping a drink in a kitchen sink, a hyena playing a concertina in an arena, or a lizard shaking its gizzard in a blizzard instead of the way chosen in this volume. In "Das Böhmische Dorf," similarly, Morgenstern says in the poem itself that Korf appears in the poem merely "because of the rhyme" with Dorf. And in "Drei Hasen" Morgenstern asks to be excused from "explaining" and be allowed to make poetry for its own sake: "Wer fragt, der ist gerichtet, hier wird nicht kommentiert, hier wird an sich gedichtet." [14]

Occasionally, when pressed hard, he gave an indication of what he had in mind with some of his

[13] Professor Wolfgang Kayser of Göttingen University in a lecture at the University of California, Berkeley, May, 1956.
[14] Christian Morgenstern, *Egon und Emilie* (München: R. Piper-Verlag, 1950), p. 94.

verses. "The 'Rehlein' are nothing more than an expression of phonetics and an impression of nature—no Nietzschean profundity, O you profound interpreters! . . . Just visualize the first and last lines mumbled by one of the gallows gang, and the intermediate 'nine,' 'ten,' etc. by a second, third, and so forth—all this in a sort of meditative trance, such as might be expected from these fellows." [15] The moonsheep, he says, might be thought of as the moon itself—first on the wide expanse of the firmament, later vanishing behind mountains, in a "dream" seeing his tiny body as the universe, and appearing as a white disc in the morning. Raven Ralph dies because he eats gallows' food—dead flesh. Fishes are dumb, hence their song ("the profoundest German poem") [16] can only be expressed in dumb symbols.[17] Symbolism? Allegory? Subtle meanings? "If I may advise: Just have the innocence to enjoy yourself." [18] Elsewhere Morgenstern says: "I have often been asked what was my purpose when I wrote the Galgenlieder. Well, originally, none but my own enjoyment and that of some other young fools. Later their audience expanded and so did their artistic purpose. But even now no satirical or philosophical purpose should be injected; rather, the reader should experience the seeing, sensing, and feeling from which the verses sprang. They aim at relaxation for contemporary man; hemmed in by scholars and their slogans, and hence confined to dead-end streets, he might breathe more freely in an atmosphere in which the oppressive heaviness of our humorless scientific era is shaken off or turned upside down. Besides aiming at relaxation the verses

[15] *Ueber die Galgenlieder*, pp. 9, 13.
[16] *Ibid.*, p. 37.
[17] *Ibid.*, p. 14.
[18] *Ibid.*, p. 9.

attempt to lure our cornered and restricted imagination into an arena where it can roam at liberty." [19]

Some parts of his tongue-in-cheek "explanations" contained in *Ueber die Galgenlieder* [20] are so worded that they almost sound as though they mean what they say. Might he not really have had Helios's horses in the back of his mind when he wrote about the "silver horses" at the dawning of day in the "Chorus of the Gallows Gang"? And could not "Wentall," where "the author took the liberty of isolating two words and elevating them into a new noun," really be thought of as "somebody deep in thought, a dreamer"? On the other hand, Morgenstern clearly pulls the reader's leg when he, with pseudo-scholarly seriousness, "explains" the "Knee" as the "restless stride of the good principle after being almost destroyed." An interesting "deeper meaning" has been suggested recently: "The 'Knee' shows the whole 'glory' of a Prussian military parade. The chorus represents the senseless repetition of the movement of marching legs." [21]

During Morgenstern's time and later, the Galgenlieder were often classified as nonsense poetry. To this, Morgenstern, who was a mild-mannered, almost timid person, says, please don't, in a disarming plea to his critics: "One thing I beg of you. Should the terms 'nonsense' or 'gibberish' be included in the review—no matter how flattering the qualifying adjectives might be—kindly reconsider them in favor of something like 'folly' or 'craziness.' Surely you would not want to tag with these two evil German Philistine and tavern terms of thoughtlessness the very humor that aims at a certain kind of spir-

[19] *Ibid.*, pp. 16, 17.
[20] *Ibid.*, pp. 23–58.
[21] Hiebel, *op. cit.*, p. 185.

ituality. 'Higher nonsense' 'fit to be classified as literature' is the cheapest and unwisest that can be said" about the Galgenlieder—a slogan used without doing justice to the evidence.[22]

Christian Otto Josef Wolfgang Morgenstern was born May 6, 1871, the son of a North-German Protestant father and a South-German Catholic mother. He attended the "humanistische Gymnasium" in Breslau and studied law and economics at the university there, but practiced neither; he devoted his life, until his early death in Meran on March 9, 1914, to literature. The Galgenlieder are merely offshoots ("bloss Beiwerkchen, Nebensachen" [23] as he wrote) of his spiritual and mystic poems, which were influenced by the anthroposophy of Rudolf Steiner. His serious poems are often bracketed with those of Rilke, Dehmel, and Hofmannsthal. Yet it was the Galgenlieder that made Morgenstern famous.

Because of the Galgenlieder's dependence on the German language, they have been said to defy translation.[24] In the present collection, some poems based on puns were translated by trying a similar pun (e.g., "Das Gebet"), others were rendered by analogy— by an experimental "approach" (e.g., "Der Wer-

[22] *Ueber die Galgenlieder*, pp. 12, 13.
[23] *Ibid.*, p. 15.
[24] "Morgenstern ranks very high among modern German poets, but his international reputation is severely handicapped by the fact that many of his best works are practically untranslatable": *Cassell's Encyclopaedia of World Literature* (New York: Funk and Wagnalls, 1954), II, 1266. "Morgenstern's parodies, punning, and satiric truculence succeeded in creating an Alice-in-Wonderland climate which endeared him to millions of readers throughout the German-speaking world, but which, of course, defies translation": Angel Flores, ed., *An Anthology of German Poetry* (New York: Doubleday, 1960), p. 300.

wolf"). With one exception, difficulty of translating was not a consideration in selecting the poems for this volume—unless it was an inducement to try. The exception was "Die Nähe" which I would have loved to add, but no draft (e.g., matt-er, mattress) seemed wholly satisfactory; may a better man crack this one.[25] Otherwise I selected simply those poems that I found tempting. No complete volume of translations exists or would seem challenging enough to be attempted. The present volume offers the largest number of poems in English, the larger number of them translated for the first time. If the wisdom of including some of them was doubted by the translator himself, he was encouraged by Morgenstern's generous comment: "Great originals shine even through awkward translations." [26] Translations of individual poems have appeared in scattered publications: the first ones, to my knowledge, by B. Q. Morgan, in *Books Abroad*, XII (1938), 288–291; the latest, in *New World Writing* (New

[25] Karl F. Ross (see Acknowledgments) offers this "approach":

Die Nähe ging verträumt umher . . .	A Flat was moodily depressed;
Sie kam nie zu den Dingen selber.	one never called it sharp or curvy.
Ihr Antlitz wurde gelb und gelber,	It felt as if beset with scurvy
und ihren Leib ergriff die Zehr.	and nursed resentment in its chest.
Doch eines Nachts, derweil sie schlief,	One night, though, as it lay in bed,
da trat wer an ihr Bette hin	the hero of our narrative
und sprach: "Steh auf, mein Kind, ich bin	awakened it: "I am," he said,
der kategorische Komparativ!	"the categoric comparative.
Ich werde dich zum Näher steigern,	I'll elevate you to a Flatter
ja, wenn du willst, zur Näherin!"	or to a Flatterer, indeed!"
Die Nähe, ohne sich zu weigern,	The Flat assumed it did not matter,
sie nahm auch dies als Schicksal hin.	considered briefly and agreed.
Als Näherin jedoch vergaß	As Flatterer the Flat, however,
sie leider völlig, was sie wollte,	forgot its grievance rather fast,
und nähte Putz und hiess Frau Nolte	for everyone now finds it clever
und hielt all Obiges für Spaß.	and disregards its shallow past.

[26] Morgenstern, *Stufen*, p. 81.

York and Philadelphia: J. P. Lippincott, 1962); a small volume of English translations appeared in Germany (A. E. W. Eitzen, *The Moonsheep*, Wiesbaden: Insel-Verlag, 1953). Morgenstern had few illusions about translating. On the occasion of Ibsen's seventieth birthday, Morgenstern—the translator of *Peer Gynt*—wrote to the Copenhagen daily *Politiken:* "There is no such thing as a good or better translation of poetry from another language—there are only poor and less poor renderings." [27]

Still, the attempt to translate Morgenstern, that enfant terrible of German verse, has been made because there must be many among his German-speaking followers—that community, resembling a secret order, to whom his bizarre world forms a general background for their daily lives—who know enough English to share my own puckish enjoyment in hearing this most German of all poets talk English; and because there must be many in the English-speaking world who have merely heard his name together with the information that little of his work has been translated. To this secret order and to its potential English-speaking friends, the present translations address themselves.

[27] Bauer, *op. cit.*, p. 107. Or, as Robert Frost has said: "Poetry is what disappears in translation." And Roda Roda, the Austro-Hungarian writer, facetiously maintained that a translation is good only when it is better than the original. John Ciardi of the *Saturday Review of Literature* pessimistically, realistically, and succinctly called translation "the art of failure": "what a translator tries for is no more than the best possible failure."

Das grosse Lalulā

Kroklokwafzi? Sememēmi!
Seiokrontro—prafriplo:
Bifzi, bafzi; hulalēmi:
quasti basti bo . . .
Lalu, lalu lalu lalu la!

Hontraruru miromente
zasku zes rü rü?
Entepente, leiolente
klekwapufzi lü?
lalu lalu lalu lalu la!

Simarar kos malzipempu
silzuzankunkrei (;)!
Marjomar dos: Quempu Lempu
Siri Suri Sei []!
Lalu lalu lalu lalu la!

INTRODUCTORY POEMS

Der Lattenzaun

Es war einmal ein Lattenzaun,
mit Zwischenraum, hindurchzuschaun.

Ein Architekt, der dieses sah,
stand eines Abends plötzlich da—

und nahm den Zwischenraum heraus
und baute draus ein großes Haus.

Der Zaun indessen stand ganz dumm,
mit Latten ohne was herum.

Ein Anblick gräßlich und gemein.
Drum zog ihn der Senat auch ein.

Der Architekt jedoch entfloh
nach Afri- od- Ameriko.

The Picket Fence

One time there was a picket fence
with space to gaze from hence to thence.

An architect who saw this sight
approached it suddenly one night,

removed the spaces from the fence
and built of them a residence.

The picket fence stood there dumbfounded
with pickets wholly unsurrounded,

a view so loathsome and obscene,
the Senate had to intervene.

The architect, however, flew
to Afri- or Americoo.

Das aesthetische
Wiesel

Ein Wiesel
sass auf einem Kiesel
inmitten Bachgeriesel.

Wißt ihr
weshalb?

Das Mondkalb
verriet es mir
im Stillen:

Das raffinier-
te Tier
tat's um des Reimes willen.

The Aesthetic
Weasel

A weasel
perched on an easel
within a patch of teasel.

But why
and how?

The Moon Cow
whispered her reply
one time:

The sopheest-
icated beest
just did it for the rhyme.

Denkmalswunsch

Setze mir ein Denkmal, cher,
ganz aus Zucker, tief im Meer.

Ein Süßwassersee, zwar kurz,
werd ich dann nach meinem Sturz;

doch so lang, daß Fische, hundert,
nehmen einen Schluck verwundert.—

Diese ißt in Hamburg und
Bremen dann des Menschen Mund.—

Wiederum in eure Kreise
komm ich so auf gute Weise,

während, werd ich Stein und Erz,
nur ein Vogel seinen Sterz

oder gar ein Mensch von Wert
seinen Witz auf mich entleert.

Desire for a Monument

Set a monument for me,
built of sugar, in the sea.

It will melt, of course, and make
briefly a sweet-water lake;

meanwhile, fishes by the score
take surprised a sip or more.

They, in various ports, will then
be, in turn, consumed by men.

This way I will join the chain
of humanity again,

while, were I of stone or steel,
just some pigeon ungenteel,

or perhaps a Ph.D.
would discharge his wit on me.

Das Gebet

Die Rehlein beten zur Nacht,
  hab acht!

Halb neun!

Halb zehn!

Halb elf!

Halb zwölf!

Zwölf!

Die Rehlein beten zur Nacht,
  hab acht!
Sie falten die kleinen Zehlein,
  die Rehlein.

The Does' Prayer

The does, as the hour grows late,
        med-it-ate;

med-it-nine;

med-i-ten;

med-eleven;

med-twelve;

mednight!

The does, as the hour grows late,
        meditate.
They fold their little toesies,
        the doesies.

Im Anfang lebte, wie bekannt,
als größter Säuger der Gig-ant.

Wobei gig eine Zahl ist, die
es nicht mehr gibt,—so groß war sie!

Doch jene Größe schwand wie Rauch.
Zeit gab's genug—und Zahlen auch.

Bis eines Tags, ein winzig Ding,
der Zwölef-ant das Reich empfing.

Wo blieb sein Reich? Wo blieb er selb?—
Sein Bein wird im Museum gelb.

Zwar gab die gütige Natur
den Elef-anten uns dafur.

Doch ach, der Pulverpavian,
der Mensch voll Gier nach seinem Zahn,

erschießt ihn, statt ihm Zeit zu lassen,
zum Zehen-anten zu verblassen.

O "Klub zum Schutz der wilden Tiere",
hilf, daß der Mensch nicht ruiniere

die Sprossen dieser Riesenleiter,
die stets noch weiter führt und weiter!

Anto-logy

Of yore, on earth was dominant
the biggest mammal: the Gig-ant.

("Gig" is a numeral so vast,
it's been extinct for ages past.)

But off, like smoke, that vastness flew.
Time did abound, and numbers too,

until one day a tiny thing,
the Tweleph-ant, was chosen king.

Where is he now? Where is his throne?
In the museum pales his bone.

True, Mother Nature gave with grace
the Eleph-ant us in his place,

but, woe, that shooting anthropoid
called "Man," in quest for tusks destroyed

him ere he could degenerate,
by stages, to a Ten-ant's state.

O noble club, SPCA,
don't let Man wholly take away

the steps of that titanic scale
that leads still farther down the trail.

Wie dankbar wird der Ant dir sein,
lässt du ihn wachsen und gedeihn,—

bis er dereinst im Nebel hinten
als Nulel-ant wird stumm verschwinden.

How grateful will the Ant survive
if left to flourish and to thrive,

until he, in a far-off year,
as Zero-ant will disappear.

Gespräch einer Hausschnecke
mit sich selbst

Soll i aus meim Hause raus
Soll i aus meim Hause nit raus?
Einen Schritt raus?
Lieber nit raus?
Hausenitraus—
Hauseraus
Hauseritraus
Hausenaus
Rauserauserauserause . . . . .

(Die Schnecke verfängt sich in ihren eigenen Gedanken
oder vielmehr diese gehen mit ihr dermaßen durch, dass sie
die weitere Entscheidung der Frage verschieben muß.)

The Snail's Monologue

Shall I dwell in my shell?
Shall I not dwell in my shell?
Dwell in shell?
Rather not dwell?
Shall I not dwell,
shall I dwell,
dwell in shell
shall I shell,
shallIshellIshallIshellIshallI . . . ?

(The snail gets so entangled with his thoughts or, rather, the thoughts run away with him so that he must postpone the decision.)

Fisches Nachtgesang

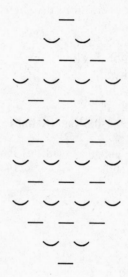

Fish's Night Song

Die Trichter

Zwei Trichter wandeln durch die Nacht.
Durch ihres Rumpfs verengten Schacht
fließt weißes Mondlicht
still und heiter
auf ihren
Waldweg
u. s.
w.

The Funnels
[TWO VERSIONS]

Two funnels travel through the night;
a sylvan moon's canescent light
employs their bodies' narrow
flue in shining pale
and cheerful
thro

ug

h

.

A funnel ambles through the night.
Within its body, moonbeams white
converge as they
descend upon
its forest
pathway
and
so
on
.

Die unmögliche Tatsache

Palmström, etwas schon an Jahren,
wird an einer Straßenbeuge
und von einem Kraftfahrzeuge
überfahren.

"Wie war" (spricht er, sich erhebend
und entschlossen weiterlebend)
"möglich, wie dies Unglück, ja— :
daß es überhaupt geschah?

"Ist die Staatskunst anzuklagen
in Bezug auf Kraftfahrwagen?
Gab die Polizeivorschrift
hier dem Fahrer freie Trift?

"Oder war vielmehr verboten,
hier Lebendige zu Toten
umzuwandeln,—kurz und schlicht:
Durfte hier der Kutscher nicht—?"

Eingehüllt in feuchte Tücher,
prüft er die Gesetzesbücher
und ist alsobald im Klaren:
Wagen durften dort nicht fahren!

Und er kommt zu dem Ergebnis:
Nur ein Traum war das Erlebnis.
Weil, so schliesst er messerscharf,
nicht sein *kann*, was nicht sein *darf*.

The Impossible Fact

Palmstroem, old, an aimless rover,
walking in the wrong direction
at a busy intersection
is run over.

"How," he says, his life restoring
and with pluck his death ignoring,
"can an accident like this
ever happen? What's amiss?

"Did the state administration
fail in motor transportation?
Did police ignore the need
for reducing driving speed?

"Isn't there a prohibition,
barring motorized transmission
of the living to the dead?
Was the driver right who sped . . . ?"

Tightly swathed in dampened tissues
he explores the legal issues,
and it soon is clear as air:
Cars were not permitted there!

And he comes to the conclusion:
His mishap was an illusion,
for, he reasons pointedly,
that which *must* not, *can* not be.

Auf dem Fliegenplaneten

Auf dem Fliegenplaneten,
da geht es dem Menschen nicht gut:
Denn was er hier der Fliege,
die Fliege dort ihm tut.

An Bändern voll Honig kleben
die Menschen dort allesamt
und andre sind zum Verleben
in süßlichem Bier verdammt.

In einem nur scheinen die Fliegen
dem Menschen vorauszustehn:
Man bäckt uns nicht in Semmeln
noch trinkt man uns aus Versehn.

At the Housefly Planet

Upon the housefly planet
the fate of the human is grim:
for what he does here to the housefly,
the fly does there unto him.

To paper with honey cover
the humans there adhere,
while others are doomed to hover
near death in vapid beer.

However, one practice of humans
the flies will not undertake:
they will not bake us in muffins
nor swallow us by mistake.

Der Schnupfen

Ein Schnupfen hockt auf der Terrasse,
auf dass er sich ein Opfer fasse

—und stürzt alsbald mit großem Grimm
auf einen Menschen namens Schrimm.

Paul Schrimm erwidert prompt: Pitschü!
und *hat* ihn drauf bis Montag früh.

The Sniffle

A sniffle crouches on the terrace
in wait for someone he can harass.

And suddenly he jumps with vim
upon a man by name of Schrimm.

Paul Schrimm, responding with "hatchoo,"
is stuck with him the weekend through.

Golch und Flubis

Golch und Flubis, das sind zwei
Gaukler aus der Titanei,

die mir einst in einer Nacht
Zri, die große Zra vermacht.

Mangelt irgend mir ein Ding,
ein Beweis, ein Baum, ein Ring—

ruf ich Golch und er verwandelt
sich in das, worum sich's handelt.

Während Flubis umgekehrt
das wird, was man gern entbehrt.

Bei z.B. Halsbeschwerden
wird das Halsweh Flubis werden.

Fällte dich z.B. Mord,
ging' der Tod als Flubis fort.

Lieblich lebt es sich mit solchen
wackern Flubissen und Golchen.

Darum suche jeder ja
dito Zri, die große Zra.

Golch and Flubis

Golch and Flubis, these are two
sorcerers from Shangri-loo

who, one night, were given me
by the mighty Zra queen, Zri.

If I lack a certain thing,
—say, a proof, a tree, a ring—

I call Golch, who will with speed
change himself to what I need.

Flubis, contrary to this,
turns to what one wants to miss.

If a painful throat your plight is,
Flubis flees as laryngitis.

If a slayer stabbed your heart,
Flubis would as Death depart.

Life's a lark, indeed, when these
Golches help and Flubises.

Fortunate, therefore, is he
who wins grace from Zra queen Zri.

GALLOWS HILL

Galgenberg

Blödem Volke unverständlich
treiben wir des Lebens Spiel.
Grade das, was unabwendlich
fruchtet unserm Spott als Ziel.

Magst es Kinder-Rache nennen
an des Daseins tiefem Ernst;
wirst das Leben besser kennen,
wenn du uns verstehen lernst.

Gallows Hill

Enigmatic for the masses
playfully with life we fool.
That which human wits surpasses
draws our special ridicule.

Call it infantile vendetta
on life's deeply serious aim—
you will know existence better
once you understand our game.

Bundeslied der Galgenbrüder

O schauerliche Lebenswirrn,
wir hängen hier am roten Zwirn!
Die Unke unkt, die Spinne spinnt,
und schiefe Scheitel kämmt der Wind.

O Greule, Greule, wüste Greule!
Du bist verflucht! so sagt die Eule.
Der Sterne Licht am Mond zerbricht.
Doch dich zerbrach's noch immer nicht.

O Greule, Greule, wüste Greule!
Hört ihr den Huf der Silbergäule?
Es schreit der Kauz: pardauz! pardauz!
da taut's, da graut's, da braut's, da blaut's!

Chorus of the Gallows Gang

O life of horror-stricken dread!
We dangle from the crimson thread.
The spider spins, the croaker croaks,
and crookèd curls the nightwind strokes.

O growl, O growl, O rumbling growl!
Damned are your spirits, quoth the owl.
The starlight pales before the moon.
Will you yourself be paling soon?

O growl, O growl, O rumbling growl!
You hear the silver horses prowl?
The hooter hoots his weird hoo-hoos.
It dawns and dews and brews and blues.

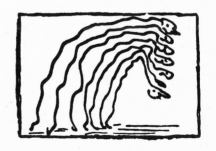

47

Galgenbruders Lied
an Sophie, die Henkersmaid

Sophie, mein Henkersmädel,
komm, küsse mir den Schädel!
Zwar ist mein Mund
ein schwarzer Schlund—
doch du bist gut und edel!

Sophie, mein Henkersmädel,
komm, streichle mir den Schädel!
Zwar ist mein Haupt
des Haars beraubt—
doch du bist gut und edel!

Sophie, mein Henkersmädel,
komm, schau mir in den Schädel!
Die Augen zwar,
sie fraß der Aar—
doch du bist gut und edel!

The Hanged Man's Song
to the Hangman's Maid

Sophia, hangman's mate,
O come and kiss my pate!
My mouth now is
a black abyss—
but you are nobly great!

Sophia, hangman's mate,
O come, caress my pate!
My skull is bare
and lacking hair—
but you are nobly great!

Sophia, hangman's mate,
O come, behold my pate!
The eagle flies—
he picked my eyes.
But you are nobly great.

Nein!

Pfeift der Sturm?
Keift ein Wurm?
Heulen
Eulen
hoch vom Turm?

Nein!

Es ist des Galgenstrickes
dickes
Ende, welches ächzte,
gleich als ob
im Galopp
eine müdgehetzte Mähre
nach dem nächsten Brunnen lechzte
(der vielleicht noch ferne wäre).

Nay!

Shrieks the gale?
Squeaks the snail?
Howls
an owl's
Hoo-hoot from jail?

Nay!

It is the gallows' loose
noose
with its heavy end a-rasping,
just as though
on the go
an exhausted, panting steed
for the nearest trough were gasping
(which might still be far indeed).

Galgenkindes Wiegenlied

Schlaf, Kindlein, schlaf,
am Himmel steht ein Schaf;
das Schaf, das ist aus Wasserdampf
und kämpft wie du den Lebenskampf.
Schlaf, Kindlein, schlaf.

Schlaf, Kindlein, schlaf,
die Sonne frißt das Schaf,
sie leckt es weg vom blauen Grund
mit langer Zunge, wie ein Hund.
Schlaf, Kindlein, schlaf.

Schlaf, Kindlein, schlaf.
Nun ist es fort, das Schaf.
Es kommt der Mond und schilt sein Weib;
die läuft ihm weg, das Schaf im Leib.
Schlaf, Kindlein, schlaf.

Gallows Child's Lullaby

Sleep, baby, sleep,
there's in the sky a sheep;
the sheep is made of cloud and dew
and fights life's battle just like you.
Sleep, baby, sleep.

Sleep, baby, sleep,
the sun eats up the sheep,
he laps it from the azure ground
with tongue extended like a hound.
Sleep, baby, sleep.

Sleep, baby, sleep.
Now it is gone, the sheep.
The moon appears and starts to chide
her mate who runs, the sheep inside.
Sleep, baby, sleep.

Wie sich das Galgenkind die Monatsnamen merkt

Jaguar
Zebra
Nerz
Mandrill
Maikäfer
Ponny
Muli
Auerochs
Wespenbär
Locktauber
Robbenbär
Zehenbär.

How the Gallows Child Remembers
the Names of the Months

Jaguary
Cassowary
Marten
Mandrill
Maybird
Coon
Shoofly
Locust
Serpent bear
Octopus
North Pole bear
Remem bear

Der Mond

Als Gott den lieben Mond erschuf,
gab er ihm folgenden Beruf:

Beim Zu- sowohl wie beim Abnehmen
sich deutschen Lesern zu bequemen,

ein a formierend und ein g —
daß keiner groß zu denken hätt'.

Befolgend dies ward der Trabant
ein völlig deutscher Gegenstand.

The Moon

When God had made the moon on high,
He did as follows specify:

while waning, waxing overhead,
her phase in German should be read,

an *a* describing and a *g*
(read "Ab" and "Zu" in Germany).

And thus became what shines at night
a purely German satellite.

Der Seufzer

Ein Seufzer lief Schlittschuh auf nächtlichem Eis
und träumte von Liebe und Freude.
Es war an dem Stadtwall, und schneeweiß
glänzten die Stadtwallgebäude.

Der Seufzer dacht' an ein Maidelein
und blieb erglühend stehen.
Da schmolz die Eisbahn unter ihm ein—
und er sank—und ward nimmer gesehen.

The Sigh

A sigh went a-skating on ice in the night,
    of love and of joy he was dreaming.
The scene was the town wall, and snow white
    the town wall's mansions were gleaming.

The sigh, he thought of a maiden fair,
    and a-glowing he stopped on the scene.
That melted the ice below him there
    and he sank—and was nevermore seen.

Der Rabe Ralf

Der Rabe Ralf
    will will hu hu
dem niemand half
    still still du du
half sich allein
am Rabenstein
    will will still still
      hu hu

Die Nebelfrau
    will will hu hu
nimmt's nicht genau
    still still du du
sie sagt nimm nimm
's ist nicht so schlimm
    will will still still
      hu hu

Doch als ein Jahr
    will will hu hu
vergangen war
still still du du
da lag im Rot
der Rabe tot
    will will still still
      du du

The Raven Ralph
[WHO ATE GALLOWS FOOD]

> The Raven Ralph
>   will will hoo hoo,
> he halped himsalf
>   still still do do
> all on his own
> at Raven's Stone
>   will will still still
>   hoo hoo.
>
> The Maid of Mist
>   will will hoo hoo
> knows every twist
>   still still do do
> "Take, take," said she,
> " 'tis all for free."
> Will will still still
>   hoo hoo.
>
> But when at last
>   will will hoo hoo
> a year had passed
>   still still do do
> the sun rose red,
> and Ralph lay dead
>   will will still still
>   do do.

K.F.R.

Das Knie

Ein Knie geht einsam durch die Welt.
Es ist ein Knie, sonst nichts!
Es ist kein Baum! Es ist kein Zelt!
Es ist ein Knie, sonst nichts.

Im Kriege ward einmal ein Mann
erschossen um und um.
Das Knie allein blieb unverletzt—
als wär's ein Heiligtum.

Seitdem geht's einsam durch die Welt.
Es ist ein Knie, sonst nichts.
Es ist kein Baum, es ist kein Zelt.
Es ist ein Knie sonst nichts.

The Knee

On earth there roams a lonely knee.
It's just a knee, that's all.
It's not a tent, it's not a tree,
it's just a knee, that's all.

In battle, long ago, a man
was riddled through and through.
The knee alone escaped unhurt
as if it were taboo.

Since then there roams a lonely knee,
it's just a knee, that's all.
It's not a tent, it's not a tree,
it's just a knee, that's all.

Der Schaukelstuhl
auf der verlassenen Terrasse

"Ich bin ein einsamer Schaukelstuhl
und wackel im Winde, im Winde.

Auf der Terrasse, da ist es kuhl,
und ich wackel im Winde, im Winde.

Und ich wackel und nackel den ganzen Tag.
Und es nackelt und rackelt die Linde.
Wer weiß, was sonst wohl noch wackeln mag
im Winde, im Winde, im Winde."

The Rocking Chair
on the Deserted Terrace

"I am a lonely rocking chair
and I swing in the breeze, in the breeze.

Out on the terrace, so c–o–o–o–l is the air,
and I swing in the breeze, in the breeze.

And I'm swinging and swaying the live long day,
as are swaying and playing the trees.
Who knows, I wonder, what else may sway
in the breeze, in the breeze, in the breeze."

Galgenbruders Frühlingslied

Es lenzet auch auf unserm Spahn,
o selige Epoche!
Ein Hälmlein will zum Lichte nahn
aus einem Astwurmloche.

Es schaukelt bald im Winde hin
und schaukelt bald drin her.
Mir ist beinah, ich wäre wer,
der ich doch nicht mehr bin . . .

Gallows Brother's Spring Song

It's springtide at my gallows' beams!
O time of joy and blessing!
A bladelet in a knothole dreams
of sunlight's sweet caressing.

The breezes rock it tenderly,
they rock it to and fro—
I almost feel alive, although
I am no longer me.

Das Hemmed

Kennst du das einsame Hemmed?
Flattertata, flattertata.

Der's trug ist baß verdämmet!
Flattertata, flattertata.

Es knattert und rattert im Winde.
Windurudei, windurudei.

Es weint wie ein kleines Kinde.
Windurudei, windurudei.

Das ist das einsame
Hemmed.

Song of the Derelict Shirt

Know ye the derelict shirret?
Fluttera-tah, fluttera-tah.

He's damned who used to wear it!
Fluttera-tah, fluttera-tah.

It's chucked and it's plucked by the gale.
Winduru-deye, winduru-deye.

It whines with a babyish wail.
Winduru-deye, winduru-deye.

That is the derelict
shirret.

CHRISTIAN'S ZOO

Der Sperling und das Känguru

In seinem Zaun das Känguru—
es hockt und guckt dem Sperling zu.

Der Sperling sitzt auf dem Gebäude—
doch ohne sonderliche Freude.

Vielmehr, er fühlt, den Kopf geduckt,
wie ihn das Känguru beguckt.

Der Sperling sträubt den Federflaus—
die Sache ist auch gar zu kraus.

Ihm ist, als ob er kaum noch säße . . .
Wenn nun das Känguru ihn fräße ?!

Doch dieses dreht nach einer Stunde
den Kopf, aus irgend einem Grunde,

vielleicht auch ohne tiefern Sinn,
nach einer andern Richtung hin.

The Sparrow and the Kangaroo

Behind the fence, the kangaroo
has on a sparrow cast his view.

The sparrow perches on the pale—
he doesn't feel too hap and hale.

Uneasily he feels, instead,
the mammal's gaze and ducks his head.

The sparrow ruffles up his wings—
he doesn't trust the looks of things.

A terror threatens to unseat him:
What if the kangaroo should eat him?

The latter, though, will briefly pause,
then turn his head, perhaps for cause

(or possibly without reflection)
unto a different direction.

Das Nasobēm

Auf seinen Nasen schreitet
einher das Nasobēm,
von seinem Kind begleitet.
Es steht noch nicht im Brehm.

Es steht noch nicht im Meyer.
Und auch im Brockhaus nicht.
Es trat aus meiner Leier
zum ersten Mal ans Licht.

Auf seinen Nasen schreitet
(wie schon gesagt) seitdem,
von seinem Kind begleitet,
einher das Nasobēm.

The Nosobame

Upon his noses stalketh
around—the Nosobame;
with him, his offspring walketh.
He is not yet in Brehm,

you find him not in Meyer
nor does him Brockhaus cite.
He stepped forth from my lyre
the first time into light.

Upon his noses stalketh
—I will again proclaim—
(with him his offspring walketh),
since then, the Nosobame.

Die Schildkrökröte

"Ich bin nun tausend Jahre alt
und werde täglich älter;
der Gotenkönig Theobald
erzog mich im Behälter.

Seitdem ist mancherlei geschehn,
doch weiß ich nichts davon;
zur Zeit, da lässt für Geld mich sehn
ein Kaufmann zu Heilbronn.

Ich kenne nicht des Todes Bild
und nicht des Sterbens Nöte:
Ich bin die Schild- ich bin die Schild-
Ich bin die Schild-krö-kröte."

The Tortoitoise

"I am a thousand seasons old
and getting on in age;
the Gothic ruler Theobold
confined me in a cage.

A lot has happened since that day,
but what, I do not know.
At present I am on display,
for money, in a show.

All talk of death I can ignore
as so much empty noise.
I am the tor-, I am the tor-,
I am the tor-toi-toise."

Das Huhn

In der Bahnhofhalle, nicht für es gebaut,
geht ein Huhn
hin und her . . .
Wo, wo ist der Herr Stationsvorsteh'r?
Wird dem Huhn
man nichts tun?
Hoffen wir es ! Sagen wir es laut:
daß ihm unsre Sympathie gehört,
selbst an dieser Stätte, wo es—"stört"!

The Hen

In the railroad station, never built for her,
walks a hen
to and fro.
Where, where did the station master go?
Will not men
harm the hen?
Let's hope *not*. Let's candidly aver
that our sympathy she still enjoys,
even in this place, where she annoys.

Die Beichte des Wurms

Es lebt in einer Muschel
ein Wurm gar seltner Art;
der hat mir mit Getuschel
sein Herze offenbart.

Sein armes kleines Herze,
hei, wie das flog und schlug!
Ihr denket wohl, ich scherze?
Ach, denket nicht so klug.

Es lebt in einer Muschel
ein Wurm gar seltner Art;
der hat mir mit Getuschel
sein Herze offenbart.

The Worm's Confession

There lives inside a mussel
a worm so wondrously;
he has with gentle bustle
revealed his heart to me.

It pounded, never resting,
that aching little heart!
You think that I am jesting?
O don't think you're so smart.

There lives inside a mussel
a worm so wondrously;
he has with gentle bustle
revealed his heart to me.

Ein finstrer Esel sprach einmal
zu seinem ehlichen Gemahl:

"Ich bin so dumm, du bist so dumm,
wir wollen sterben gehen, kumm!"

Doch wie es kommt so öfter eben:
Die beiden blieben fröhlich leben.

The Two Donkeys

A gloomy donkey, tir'd of life
one day addressed his wedded wife:

"I am so dumb, you are so dumb,
let's go and die together, come!"

But as befalls, time and again,
they lived on happily, the twain.

Möwenlied

Die Möwen sehen alle aus,
als ob sie Emma hiessen.
Sie tragen einen weissen Flaus
und sind mit Schrot zu schießen.

Ich schieße keine Möwe tot,
ich laß sie lieber leben—
und füttre sie mit Roggenbrot
und rötlichen Zibeben.

O Mensch, du wirst nie nebenbei
der Möwe Flug erreichen.
Wofern du Emma heißest, sei
zufrieden, ihr zu gleichen.

The Seagulls

The seagulls by their looks suggest
that Emma is their name;
they wear a white and fluffy vest
and are the hunter's game.

I never shoot a seagull dead;
their life I do not take.
I like to feed them gingerbread
and bits of raisin cake.

O human, you will never fly
the way the seagulls do;
but if your name is Emma, why,
be glad they look like you.

K.F.R.

Das Perlhuhn

Das Perlhuhn zählt: eins, zwei, drei, vier . . .
Was zählt es wohl, das gute Tier,
  dort unter den dunklen Erlen?

Es zählt, von Wissensdrang gejückt,
(der es sowohl wie uns entzückt):
  Die Anzahl seiner Perlen.

The Pearl Hen

The pearl hen counts: one, two, three, four . . .
What does it count forevermore
    beneath the redwood burls?

It counts with scientific zeal
(which does to *it* and *us* appeal):
    the number of its pearls.

Das Geierlamm

Der Lämmergeier ist bekannt,
das Geierlamm erst hier genannt.

Der Geier, der ist offenkundig,
das Lamm hingegen untergrundig.

Es sagt nicht hu, es sagt nicht mäh
und frißt dich auf aus nächster Näh.

Und dreht das Auge dann zum Herrn.
Und alle haben's herzlich gern.

The Hawken Chick

The Chicken Hawk is widely known;
the Hawken Chick is all my own.

The Hawk swoops down rapaciously;
the Chick does things more graciously.

It does not cluck, it does not coo;
but when you're close, it swallows you,

then stands so innocent and mute
that all are saying: "My, how cute!"

K.F.R.

Der Leu

Auf einem Wandkalenderblatt
ein Leu sich abgebildet hat.

Er blickt dich an bewegt und still
den ganzen 17. April.

Wodurch er zu erinnern liebt,
daß es ihn immerhin noch gibt.

The Lion

A leaf of a calendar on the wall
displays a lion, grand and tall.

He views you regal and serene
the whole of April seventeen.

Reminding you, lest you forget,
that he is not extinct as yet.

Das Mondschaf

Das Mondschaf steht auf weiter Flur.
Es harrt und harrt der großen Schur.
 Das Mondschaf.

Das Mondschaf rupft sich einen Halm
und geht dann heim auf seine Alm.
 Das Mondschaf.

Das Mondschaf spricht zu sich im Traum:
"Ich bin des Weltalls dunkler Raum."
 Das Mondschaf.

Das Mondschaf liegt am Morgen tot.
Sein Leib ist weiß, die Sonn' ist rot.
 Das Mondschaf.

The Moonsheep

The moonsheep stands upon the clearing.
It waits and waits to get his shearing.
    The moonsheep.

The moonsheep plucks himself a blade
returning to his alpine glade.
    The moonsheep.

"I am," the sheep says in his dream,
"the center of the cosmic scheme."
    The moonsheep.

The moonsheep, in the morn, lies dead.
His flesh is white, the sun is red.
    The moonsheep.

Schicksal

Der Wolke Zickzackzunge spricht:
ich bringe dir, mein Hammel, Licht.

Der Hammel, der im Stalle stand,
ward links und hinten schwarz gebrannt.

Sein Leben grübelt er seitdem:
warum ihm dies geschah von wem?

Fate

With zig-zag tongue, the storm cloud spake:
"To you, O ram, the light I take."

Upon his left and on his back
the ram, scorched in his barn, turns black.

Since then he racks his brain in gloom:
Why was this done to him? By whom?

Der Nachtschelm und das Siebenschwein
ODER Eine glückliche Ehe

Der Nachtschelm und das Siebenschwein,
die gingen eine Ehe ein,
    o wehe!
Sie hatten dreizehn Kinder, und
davon war eins der Schluchtenhund,
zwei andre waren Rehe.

Das vierte war die Rabenmaus,
das fünfte war ein Schneck samt Haus,
    o Wunder!
Das sechste war ein Käuzelein,
das siebte war ein Siebenschwein
und lebte in Burgunder.

Acht war ein Gürteltier nebst Gurt,
neun starb sofort nach der Geburt,
    o wehe!
Von zehn bis dreizehn ist nicht klar;
doch wie dem auch gewesen war,
es war eine glückliche Ehe!

The Nightrogue and the Sevenswine
OR A Happy Pair

The Nightrogue and the Sevenswine
in matrimony did combine,
          beware!
Soon thirteen offspring came around;
the first one was the canyonhound
and two were doesies fair.

The fourth one was the ravenmouse,
the fifth one was a snail with house,
          what sport!
A hooting owl was sixth in line,
the seventh was a sevenswine
who lived in purple port.

Eighth came an earth hog, down to earth;
the ninth died shortly after birth,
          beware!
Whatever may the fate have been
of ten, eleven, twelve, thirteen—
there was a happy pair!

Geburtsakt der Philosophie

Erschrocken staunt der Heide Schaf mich an,
als säh's in mir den ersten Menschenmann.
Sein Blick steckt an; wir stehen wie im Schlaf;
mir ist, ich säh zum ersten Mal ein Schaf.

Birth of Philosophy

The heath sheep glares at me with frightened awe
as though I were the first of men it saw.
Contagious glare! We stand as though asleep;
it seems the first time that I see a sheep.

FAIRYLAND

Die Fingur

Es lacht die Nachtalp-Henne,
es weint die Windhorn-Gans,
es bläst der schwarze Senne
zum Tanz.

Ein Uhu-Tauber turtelt
nach seiner Uhuin.
Ein kleiner Sechs-Elf hurtelt
von Busch zu Busch dahin . . .

Und Wiedergänger gehen,
und Raben rufen kolk,
und aus den Teichen sehen
die Fingur und ihr Volk . . .

The Fingoor

The nightalp chicken chuckles,
the windhorn ganders toot;
the swarthy swain unbuckles
his flute.

A he-owl, dove-like, turtles
to woo his owlish she;
a little Six Nix hurtles
along from tree to tree . . .

And spooks their spook are wreaking,
and crows are cawing "croak";
and from the ponds are peeking
the Fingoor and her folk.

K.F.R.

Der Zwölf-Elf hebt die linke Hand:
Da schlägt es Mitternacht im Land.

Es lauscht der Teich mit offnem Mund.
Ganz leise heult der Schluchtenhund.

Die Dommel reckt sich auf im Rohr.
Der Moorfrosch lugt aus seinem Moor.

Der Schneck horcht auf in seinem Haus;
desgleichen die Kartoffelmaus.

Das Irrlicht selbst macht Halt und Rast
auf einem windgebrochnen Ast.

Sophie, die Maid, hat ein Gesicht:
Das Mondschaf geht zum Hochgericht.

Die Galgenbrüder wehn im Wind.
Im fernen Dorfe schreit ein Kind.

Zwei Maulwürf küssen sich zur Stund
als Neuvermählte auf den Mund.

Hingegen tief im finstern Wald
ein Nachtmahr seine Fäuste ballt:

Dieweil ein später Wanderstrumpf
sich nicht verlief in Teich und Sumpf.

The Twelve Nix

The Twelve Nix raises up his hand
and midnight strikes throughout the land.

The gaping pond in silence harks;
the canyon canine softly barks.

The bittern rises from its bog;
out of his swampland peers the frog.

The snail perks up within his house,
and likewise the potato mouse.

The will o' wisp has stopped its jig
and rests upon a broken twig.

Sophia dreams, the hangman's wench:
The moonsheep pleads before the bench.

The gallows gang sways up and down;
an infant cries far off in town.

Two moles, just married, turn about
and kiss each other on the snout.

While deep within the forest's mist
a spiteful night ghoul shakes his fist

because a hiker, late on tour,
did not get lost in pond and moor.

Der Rabe Ralf ruft schaurig: "Kra!
Das End ist da! Das End ist da!"

Der Zwölf-Elf senkt die linke Hand:
Und wieder schläft das ganze Land.

The Raven Ralph calls out in fear:
"The end is near, the end is near!"

The Twelve Nix, now, puts down his hand
and sleep again enshrouds the land.

K.F.R.

Das Problem

Der Zwölf-Elf kam auf sein Problem
und sprach: Ich heiße unbequem.
Als hiess' ich etwa Drei-Vier
statt Sieben—Gott verzeih mir!

Und siehe da, der Zwölf-Elf nannt' sich
von jenem Tag ab Dreiundzwanzig.

The Problem
[AN APPROACH]

The Twelve Nix on his problem came
and said: I have an awkward name,
as if, perhaps, my name were One-Three
instead of Thirteen—grace upon me!

And, onward from this incident, he
has called himself One-Hundred Twenty.

K.F.R.

Die Mitternachtsmaus

Wenn's mitternächtigt und nicht Mond
noch Stern das Himmelshaus bewohnt,
läuft zwölfmal durch das Himmelshaus
die Mitternachtsmaus.

Sie pfeift auf ihrem kleinen Maul,—
im Traume brüllt der Höllengaul . . .
Doch ruhig läuft ihr Pensum aus
die Mitternachtsmaus.

Ihr Herr, der grosse weisse Geist,
ist nämlich solche Nacht verreist.
Wohl ihm! Es hütet ihm sein Haus
die Mitternachtsmaus.

The Midnight Mouse

At midnight when nor moon nor star
enthroned upon the heavens are,
thrice runs around the Heavens' House
    the Midnight Mouse.

Its little mouth gives off a peep;
the hell horse hollers in its sleep.
But never utters any grouse
    the Midnight Mouse.

Its chief, that Spirit great and white,
has gone abroad on such a night.
Fear not! For safely guards His house
    the Midnight Mouse.

K.F.R.

Ein Rabe saß auf einem Meilenstein
und rief Ka-em-zwei-ein, Ka-em-zwei-ein . . .

Der Werhund lief vorbei, im Maul ein Bein,
der Rabe rief Ka-em-zwei-ein, zwei-ein.

Vorüber zottelte das Zapfenschwein,
der Rabe rief und rief Ka-em-zwei-ein.

"Er ist besessen!"—kam man überein.
"Man führe ihn hinweg von diesem Stein!"

Zwei Hasen brachten ihn zum Kräuterdachs.
Sein Hirn war ganz verstört und weich wie Wachs.

Noch sterbend rief er (denn er starb dort) sein
Ka-em-zwei-ein, Ka-em-Ka-em-zwei-ein.

U.S. 29

A raven squatted on a highway sign
and screamed: You-ess two-nine, You-ess two-
    nine . . .

The werehound, bone in mouth, ran past to dine;
the raven screamed: You-ess two-nine, two nine.

Along the road there came the porcupine;
the raven screamed and screamed: You-ess two-nine.

"He is obsessed," the public did opine;
"he should be led away from yonder sign!"

Two rabbits carried him to Duck who quacks;
his brain was all disturbed and soft as wax.

But with his dying breath he screamed his line:
You-ess two-nine, You-ess, You-ess two-nine.

K.F.R.

Der Werwolf

Ein Werwolf eines Nachts entwich
von Weib und Kind, und sich begab
an eines Dorfschullehrers Grab
und bat ihn: Bitte, beuge mich!

Der Dorfschulmeister stieg hinauf
auf seines Blechschilds Messingknauf
und sprach zum Wolf, der seine Pfoten
geduldig kreuzte vor dem Toten:

"Der Werwolf,—sprach der gute Mann,
"des Weswolfs, Genetiv sodann,
"dem Wemwolf, Dativ, wie man's nennt,
"den Wenwolf,—damit hat's ein End'."

Dem Werwolf schmeichelten die Fälle,
er rollte seine Augenbälle.
Indessen, bat er, füge doch
zur Einzahl auch die Mehrzahl noch!

Der Dorfschulmeister aber mußte
gestehn, dass er von ihr nichts wußte.
Zwar Wölfe gäb's in großer Schar,
doch 'Wer' gäb's nur im Singular.

Der Wolf erhob sich tränenblind—
er hatte ja doch Weib und Kind!!
Doch da er kein Gelehrter eben,
so schied er dankend und ergeben.

The Banshee
[AN APPROACH]

One night, a banshee slunk away
from mate and child, and in the gloom
went to a village teacher's tomb,
requesting him: "Inflect me, pray."

The village teacher climbed up straight
upon his grave stone with its plate
and to the apparition said
who crossed his paws before the dead:

"The banSHEE, in the subject's place;
the banHERS, the possessive case.
The banHER, next, is what they call
objective case—and that is all."

The banshee marveled at the cases
and writhed with pleasure, making faces,
but said: "You did not add, so far,
the plural to the singular!"

The teacher, though, admitted then
that this was not within his ken.
"While 'bans' are frequent," he advised,
"a 'she' cannot be pluralized."

The banshee, rising clammily,
wailed: "What about my family?"
Then, being not a learned creature,
said humbly "Thanks" and left the teacher.
K.F.R.

Himmel und Erde

Der Nachtwindhund weint wie ein Kind,
dieweil sein Fell von Regen rinnt.

Jetzt jagt er wild das Neumondweib,
das hinflieht mit gebognem Leib.

Tief unten geht, ein dunkler Punkt,
querüberfeld ein Forstadjunkt.

Heaven and Earth

The nightwindhound wails like a child,
his rain-soaked hide is all defiled.

He's hunting now the newmoondame
who flees along with twisted frame.

Way down below a darkish dot
—the ranger—walks across the lot.

Die zwei Wurzeln

Zwei Tannenwurzeln groß und alt
unterhalten sich im Wald.

Was droben in den Wipfeln rauscht,
das wird hier unten ausgetauscht.

Ein altes Eichhorn sitzt dabei
und strickt wohl Strümpfe für die zwei.

Die eine sagt: knig. Die andre sagt: knag.
Das ist genug für einen Tag.

The Two Roots

A pair of pine roots, old and dark,
make conversation in the park.

The whispers where the top leaves grow
are echoed in the roots below.

An agèd squirrel sitting there
is knitting stockings for the pair.

The one says: squeak. The other: squawk.
That is enough for one day's talk.

Das Wasser

Ohne Wort, ohne Wort
rinnt das Wasser immerfort;
andernfalls, andernfalls
spräch' es doch nichts andres als:

Bier und Brot, Lieb und Treu,—
und das wäre auch nicht neu.
Dieses zeigt, dieses zeigt,
dass das Wasser besser schweigt.

The Stream

Not a word, not a word
from the flowing stream is heard.
Otherwise, otherwise
it would just soliloquize:

"Beer and bread, love so true . . ."
and this would be nothing new.
All this will, all this will
show the stream had best keep still.

Vice Versa

Ein Hase sitzt auf einer Wiese,
des Glaubens, niemand sähe diese.

Doch, im Besitze eines Zeißes,
betrachtet voll gehaltnen Fleißes

vom vis-à-vis gelegnen Berg
ein Mensch den kleinen Löffelzwerg.

Ihn aber blickt hinwiederum
ein Gott von fern an, mild und stumm.

Vice Versa

A rabbit sits upon the green
believing it can not be seen.

A man, though, with a telescope
and watching keenly on a slope

extending from a near-by knoll,
observes the little spoon-eared troll.

The man, in turn, from far is seen
by God, reposeful and serene.

Der Gingganz

Ein Stiefel wandern und sein Knecht
von Knickebühl gen Entenbrecht.

Urplötzlich auf dem Felde drauß
begehrt der Stiefel: Zieh mich aus!

Der Knecht drauf: Es ist nicht an Dem;
doch sagt mir, lieber Herre,—!: wem?

Dem Stiefel gibt es einen Ruck:
Fürwahr, beim heiligen Nepomuk,

ich GING GANZ in Gedanken hin . . .
Du weißt, dass ich ein andrer bin,

seitdem ich meinen Herrn verlor . . .
Der Knecht wirft beide Arm' empor,

als wollt er sagen: Laß doch, laß!
Und weiter zieht das Paar fürbaß.

The Wentall

A boot was walking with his jack
from Haverstraw to Hackensack.

Then, suddenly, among the trees,
the boot demanded: "Strip me, please!"

The jack replied: "Yes, Sir, why not;
but, may I ask—of whom or what?"

The boot, at that, was thunderstruck
and answered: "Holy Nepomuk!

I WENT ALL lost in thought, bemused—
you know, I have been quite confused

since I have lost my master, so . . ."
The jack threw up his arms as though

he meant to say: "Why should I care?"
And further trudged along the pair.

Bim, Bam, Bum

Ein Glockenton fliegt durch die Nacht,
als hätt' er Vogelflügel;
er fliegt in römischer Kirchentracht
wohl über Tal und Hügel.

Er sucht die Glockentönin BIM,
die ihm vorausgeflogen;
d.h. die Sache ist sehr schlimm,
sie hat ihn nämlich betrogen.

"O komm" so ruft er, "komm, dein BAM
erwartet dich voll Schmerzen.
Komm wieder, BIM, geliebtes Lamm,
dein BAM liebt dich von Herzen!"

Doch BIM, daß ihr's nur alle wisst,
hat sich dem BUM ergeben;
der ist zwar auch ein guter Christ,
allein das ist es eben.

Der BAM fliegt weiter durch die Nacht
wohl über Wald und Lichtung.
Doch, ach, er fliegt umsonst! Das macht,
er fliegt in falscher Richtung.

Ding Dong Dang

A bell sound flies through night in search,
as if on bird wings soaring;
he flies in the garb of the Roman Church,
the hills and dales exploring.

He seeks the lady bell sound DING
who'd winged away before him;
they have to settle a serious thing:
she broke the troth she swore him.

"O come," he calls, "O come. Your DONG
awaits you, pet, with anguish.
Return, my DING, for whom I long,
don't let your sweetheart languish!"

But DING had yielded, it is true,
to DANG's gallant devices;
he is an honest Christian too—
that's just what caused the crisis.

So DONG continues through the night
through bare and wooded section.
He flies, alas, in vain: His flight
is in the wrong direction.

Das Einhorn

Das Einhorn lebt von Ort zu Ort
nur noch als Wirtshaus fort.

Man geht hinein zur Abendstund'
und sitzt den Stammtisch rund.

Wer weiß! Nach Jahr und Tag sind wir
auch ganz wie jenes Tier:

Hotels nur noch, darin man speist—
(so völlig wurden wir zu Geist).

Im "Goldnen Menschen" sitzt man dann
und sagt sein Solo an . . .

The Unicorn

The unicorn has only been
preserved in signs that mark an inn.

There, round the table, one enjoys
an evening with the boys.

Who knows how soon will I and you
be like this creature too:

Just names of taverns we shall be
(spiritualized entirely).

Then in the "Golden Man" till late
one plays and draws a straight.

Naturspiel

Ein Hund,
mit braunen Flecken
auf weißem Grund,
jagt ein Huhn,
mit weißen Flecken
auf braunem Grund,
nicht unergötzlich
in einem Torgang
von links nach rechts
von rechts nach links,
herüber,
hinüber.

Plötzlich
(Gott behüte uns
vor einem ähnlichen Vorgang!)
springen
wohl im Ringen
und Reiz
der Gefechts-
leiden-
schaft,
wie im Takt—
(oh, wie kann
man
es
nur
heraus-
bringen!) . . .

Nature Spectacle

A dog
with brown markings
on white background
chases a hen
with white markings
on brown background,
not unamusingly,
in a hallway
from left to right,
from right to left,
this way,
that way.

Suddenly
(God save us
from a similar event!)
in the tumble
and jumble
of the fighting
pas-
sion,
as in one swoop—
(O, how can
one
at
all
ex-
press it!)

als wie kraft
eines gegen-
seitigen
Winks
der beiden
Eigen-
tümer—
die Flecken des Huhns
los und locker
aus ihrer Fassung
auf den Hund über
und die Flecken des Hunds
ihrerseits
auf das Huhn.

Und nun—:
(Welch ein Akt
ungestümer
reciproker
Anpassung,
mit keinem anderweitigen
Tableau
noch Prozeß
im weiten Haus,
Kreis,
Rund
und Reigen
der Natur
zu belegen!)
ist der Hund—
weiß
und das Huhn—braun
anzuschaun !!

—as if by
a mutu-
al
cue
from both
propri-
etors—
the hen's markings
jump loose and move
from their frames
onto the dog,
and the dog's markings,
in turn,
onto the hen's.

And then—
(what a phenomenon
of vigorous
reciprocal
adjustment,
documented
in no other instance
or process
in the large mansion,
circle,
sphere,
and
cycle
of nature!)
the hen
presents a brown
and the dog a white
sight!

Gruselett

Der Flügelflagel gaustert
durchs Wiruwaruwolz,
die rote Fingur plaustert
und grausig gutzt der Golz.

Scariboo

The Winglewangle phlutters
through widowadowood,
the crimson Fingoor splutters
and scary screaks the Scrood.

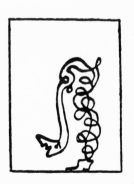

PALMSTROEM AND KORF

Palmström

Palmström steht an einem Teiche
und entfaltet groß ein rotes Taschentuch:
Auf dem Tuch ist eine Eiche
dargestellt, sowie ein Mensch mit einem Buch.

Palmström wagt nicht sich hineinzuschneuzen.
Er gehört zu jenen Käuzen,
die oft unvermittelt-nackt
Ehrfurcht vor dem Schönen packt.

Zärtlich faltet er zusammen,
was er eben erst entbreitet.
Und kein Fühlender wird ihn verdammen,
weil er ungeschneuzt entschreitet.

Palmstroem

Palmstroem stands beside a pond
where a scarlet handkerchief he wide unfolds;
on it shows an oak tree and, beyond,
a lone person and a book he holds.

Palmstroem does not dare to blow his nose;
he is plainly one of those
who at times, with sudden start,
feel a reverence for art.

He refolds with tender skill
what he just had spread out clean,
and no gentle soul will wish him ill
if, with nose unblown, he leave the scene.

Lärmschutz

Palmström liebt, sich in Geräusch zu wickeln,
teils zur Abwehr wider fremde Lärme,
teils um sich vor drittem Ohr zu schirmen.

Und so läßt er sich um seine Zimmer
Wasserröhren legen, welche brausen.
Und ergeht sich, so behütet, oft in

stundenlangen Monologen, stunden-
langen Monologen, gleich dem Redner,
von Athen, der in die Brandung brüllte,

gleich Demosthenes am Strand des Meeres.

Noise Protection

Palmstroem loves to wrap himself in noises—
partly to ward off extraneous clatter,
partly as protection against listeners.

So he has installed around his chambers
winding tubes in which the water rushes,
and indulges, thus protected, often

many hours in monologuing, many
hours in monologuing, like the ora-
tor of Athens who defied the breakers,

like Demosthenes beside the seashore.

Palmström an eine Nachtigall, die ihn nicht schlafen ließ

Möchtest du dich nicht in einen Fisch verwandeln
und gesanglich dementsprechend handeln?
Da es sonst unmöglich ist,
dass mir unternachts des Schlafes Labe
blüht, die ich nun doch notwendig habe!
Tu es, wenn du edel bist!

Deine Frau im Nest wird dich auch so bewundern,
wenn du gänzlich in der Art der Flundern
auftrittst und im Wipfel wohlig ruhst,
oder, eine fliegende Makrele
sie umflatterst, holde Philomele,
(die du mir gewiß die Liebe tust!)

Palmstroem Addressing a Nightingale
That Did Not Let Him Sleep

Can't you turn yourself into a fish
and then, songwise, act accordinglish?
Otherwise I have to be resigned
to forego, when I at night retire,
sleep's refreshing rest, which I require—
      do this, if you have a noble mind!

In your nest your spouse—you will astound her
when you, in the manner of a flounder
roost contentedly upon a tree;
or if you as flying mackerel
flit around her, lovely philomel
      (who will, certainly, do this for me).

Im Tierkostüm

Palmström liebt es, Tiere nachzuahmen,
und erzieht zwei junge Schneider
lediglich auf Tierkostüme.

So z.B. hockt er gern als Rabe
auf dem oberen Aste einer Eiche
und beobachtet den Himmel.

Häufig auch als Bernhardiner
legt er zottigen Kopf auf tapfere Pfoten,
bellt im Schlaf und träumt gerettete Wanderer.

Oder spinnt ein Netz in seinem Garten
aus Spagat und sitzt als eine Spinne
tagelang in dessen Mitte.

Oder schwimmt, ein glotzgeäugter Karpfen,
rund um die Fontäne seines Teiches
und erlaubt den Kindern ihn zu füttern.

Oder hängt sich im Kostüm des Storches
unter eines Luftschiffs Gondel
und verreist so nach Egypten.

Palmstroem in Animal Costume

Palmstroem loves to copy animal creatures.
and he trains two junior tailors
specially to make him animal costumes.

Thus, e.g., he likes to perch as raven
in the upper branches of an oak tree
and to watch there the horizon.

Often, too, as St. Bernard he
lays his shaggy head on valiant forepaws,
barks when sleeping, dreams of rescued travelers.

Or he spins a cobweb in his garden
using string, and sits there as a spider
many days within its center.

Or as carp with goggle eyes he splashes
in a circle round the fish pond's fountain
and permits the boys and girls to feed him.

Or he hangs, dressed up in stork attire,
underneath the cabin of an airship
and thus travels forth to Egypt.

Die Tagnachtlampe

Korf erfindet eine Tagnachtlampe,
die, sobald sie angedreht,
selbst den hellsten Tag
in Nacht verwandelt.

Als er sie vor des Kongresses Rampe
demonstriert, vermag
niemand, der sein Fach versteht,
zu verkennen, dass es sich hier handelt—

(Finster wird's am hellerlichten Tag,
und ein Beifallssturm das Haus durchweht)
(Und man ruft dem Diener Mampe:
"Licht anzünden")—dass es sich hier handelt

um das Faktum: dass gedachte Lampe,
in der Tat, wenn angedreht,
selbst den hellsten Tag
in Nacht verwandelt.

The Daynight Lamp

Korf invents a daynight lamp
which, as soon as operated,
turns the brightest day
into night.

When he demonstrates it on the ramp
of Convention Hall, no expert may
gainsay, if he's not opinionated,
that one finds it quite . . .

(darkness falls upon the sunlit day;
delegates are clapping, fascinated,
and one calls to Butler Bramp:
"Turn the light on!") . . . that one finds it quite

evident that the invented lamp
will indeed when operated
turn the brightest day
into night.

Korf erfindet eine Art von Witzen . . .

Korf erfindet eine Art von Witzen,
die erst viele Stunden später wirken.
Jeder hört sie an mit langer Weile.

Doch, als hätt' ein Zunder still geglommen,
wird man nachts im Bette plötzlich munter,
selig lächelnd wie ein satter Säugling.

Korf's Joke

Korf invents a novel kind of joke
which won't take effect for many hours.
Everyone is bored when first he hears it.

But he will, as though a fuse were burning,
suddenly wake up in bed at night time,
smiling sweetly like a well-fed baby.

Die Korfsche Uhr

Korf erfindet eine Uhr,
die mit zwei Paar Zeigern kreist,
und damit nach vorn nicht nur,
sondern auch nach rückwärts weist.

Zeigt sie zwei,—somit auch zehn;
zeigt sie drei,—somit auch neun;
und man braucht nur hinzusehn,
um die Zeit nicht mehr zu scheun.

Denn auf dieser Uhr von Korfen,
mit dem janushaften Lauf,
(dazu ward sie so entworfen):
hebt die Zeit sich selber auf.

Korf's Clock

Korf a kind of clock invents
where two pairs of hands go round:
one the current hour presents,
one is always backward bound.

When it's two—it's also ten;
when it's three—it's also nine.
You just look at it, and then
time gets never out of line,

for in Korf's astute invention
with its Janus-kindred stride
(which, of course, was his intention)
time itself is nullified.

Palmströms Uhr

Palmströms Uhr ist andrer Art,
reagiert mimosisch zart.

Wer sie bittet, wird empfangen.
Oft schon ist sie so gegangen,

wie man herzlich sie gebeten,
ist zurück- und vorgetreten,

eine Stunde, zwei, drei Stunden,
jenachdem sie mitempfunden.

Selbst als Uhr, mit ihren Zeiten,
will sie nicht Prinzipien reiten:

Zwar ein Werk, wie allerwärts,
doch zugleich ein Werk—mit Herz.

Palmstroem's Clock

Palmstroem's clock—a different kind—
is mimosa-like designed.

All requests are kindly heeded:
Many times the clock proceeded

at the pace that folks were urging
—slowing up or forward surging

for one hour, or two, or three,
as impelled by sympathy.

Though a timepiece, it will never
stick to petty rules, however.

Just a clockwork, slick and smart,
yet a clockwork with a heart.

Die Probe

Zu einem seltsamen Versuch
erstand ich mir ein Nadelbuch.

Und zu dem Buch ein altes zwar,
doch äußerst kühnes Dromedar.

Ein Reicher auch daneben stand,
zween Säcke Gold in jeder Hand.

Der Reiche ging alsdann herfür
und klopfte an die Himmelstür.

Drauf Petrus sprach: "Geschrieben steht,
daß ein Kamel weit eher geht

durchs Nadelöhr als du, du Heid,
durch diese Türe groß und breit!"

Ich, glaubend fest an Gottes Wort,
ermunterte das Tier sofort,

ihm zeigend hinterm Nadelöhr
ein Zuckerhörnchen als Douceur.

Und in der Tat! Das Vieh ging durch,
obzwar sich quetschend wie ein Lurch!

Der Reiche aber sah ganz stier
und sagte nichts als: "Wehe mir!"

The Test

To set up an experiment
some money I on needles spent

and on a camel which, though old,
was quite exceptionally bold.

Near me a rich man took his stand,
twain bags of gold in either hand.

The rich man did not hesitate
to knock upon the pearly gate.

St. Peter answered: "It is writ:
A needle's eye will ere permit

a camel's body to pass through
than this wide gate make way for you."

I, trusting fully God's command,
at once cajoled the creature and

displayed behind the needle'e eye
a tempting piece of sugar pie.

And so indeed! Through went the brute,
although it wiggled like a newt.

The rich man, though, stared gloomily
and said no word but: "Woe is me!"

Die Behörde

Korf erhält vom Polizeibüro
ein geharnischt Formular,
wer er sei und wie und wo.

Welchen Orts er bis anheute war,
welchen Stands und überhaupt,
wo geboren, Tag und Jahr.

Ob ihm überhaupt erlaubt,
hier zu leben und zu welchem Zweck,
wieviel Geld er hat und was er glaubt.

Umgekehrtenfalls man ihn vom Fleck
in Arrest verführen würde, und
drunter steht: Borowsky, Heck.

Korf erwidert darauf kurz und rund:
"Einer hohen Direktion
stellt sich, laut persönlichem Befund,

untig angefertigte Person
als nichtexistent im Eigen-Sinn
bürgerlicher Konvention

vor und aus und zeichnet, wennschonhin
mitbedauernd nebigen Betreff,
K o r f. (An die Bezirksbehörde in—)."

Staunend liest's der anbetroffne Chef.

The Police Inquiry

Korf gets a police chief's questionnaire,
written in a stiff, official way,
asking who he is and how and where.

At what other places did he stay,
what professional life he claims to lead,
and when born, exactly, year and day.

Furthermore, was he indeed
licensed here to live? And would he check
where he banks, and what his race and creed?

Otherwise he'll get it in the neck
and be jailed. Below are two
signatures: Borowsky, Heck.

Korf replies in short, without ado:
"Honorable gracious Sir,
after thorough personal review

it is necessary to aver
that the party signed below
does not actually occur

in conventional reality, although
he himself by self-same fact is vexed.
K o r f. (To County Office so-and-so.)"

The concerned police chief reads, perplexed.

Der eingebundene Korf

Korf läßt sich in einen Folianten einbinden,
um selben immer bei sich zu tragen;
die Rücken liegen gemeinsam hinten,
doch vorn ist das Buch auseinandergeschlagen.

So dass er, gleichsam flügelbelastet,
mit hinter den Armen flatternden Seiten
hinwandelt, oder zu anderen Zeiten
in seinen Flügeln blätternd rastet.

Book-bound Korf

Korf arranges for someone to bind him
into a folio, to carry it always around;
both backs lie jointly behind him,
but the book is unfolded in front, where not bound.
So that he travels, like wings testing,
with arms weighted down by fluttering pages,
or, at other occasions, engages
in leafing through his wings when resting.

Die Waage

Korfen glückt die Konstruierung einer
musikalischen Personenwaage,
Pfund für Pfund mit Glockenspielanlage.

Jeder Leib wird durch sein Lied bestimmt;
selbst der kleinste Mensch, anitzt geboren,
silberglöckig seine Last vernimmt.

Nur v. Korf entsendet keine Weise,
als (man weiss) nichtexistent im Sinn
abwägbarer bürgerlicher Kreise.

The Scales

Korf succeeds in cleverly constructing
weighing scales that tell the music type
of a person—sounding bell and pipe.

Every person's body has its song;
even little babies born this morning
hear their tonal weight by silver gong.

Only for von Korf no tune is played.
He's (we know) fictitious in the eyes
of the common man who can be weighed.

Bilder, die man aufhängt umgekehrt,
mit dem Kopf nach unten, Fuß nach oben,
ändern oft verwunderlich den Wert,
weil ins Reich der Phantasie erhoben.

Palmström, dem schon frühe solches kund,
füllt entsprechend eines Zimmers Wände,
und als Maler großer Gegenstände
macht er dort begeistert Fund auf Fund.

Pictures

Pictures hung in upside-down position,
upper hand reversed with lower hand,
may find unexpected recognition,
for they are transposed to fairyland.

Palmstroem knows this, and it gives him pleasure
filling walls with paintings upside down;
as himself an artist of renown
he discovers treasure after treasure.

Venus-Palmström-Anadyomene

Palmström wünscht sich manchmal aufzulösen,
wie ein Salz in einem Glase Wasser,
so nach Sonnenuntergang besonders.

Möchte ruhen so bis Sonnenaufgang,
und dann wieder aus dem Wasser steigen—
Venus-Palmström-Anadyomene . . .

Palmstroem—Foam-begotten Aphrodite

Palmstroem sometimes wishes to dissolve
like a salt grain in a glass of water,
after sundown most particularly.

Wants to rest thus till the sun arises
and emerge thereafter from the waters—
Palmstroem, foam-begotten Aphrodite . . .

Gleichnis

Palmström schwankt als wie ein Zweig im Wind . . .
Als ihn Korf befrägt, warum er schwanke, .
meint er: weil ein lieblicher Gedanke,
wie ein Vogel, zärtlich und geschwind,
auf ein kleines ihn belastet habe—
schwanke er als wie ein Zweig im Wind,
schwingend noch von der willkommnen Gabe . . .

Simile

Palmstroem sways like foliage in the breeze . . .
When Korf asks the reason for his swaying,
he replies: A lovely thought was weighing
down upon him, tender and with ease
like a bird in delicate commotion—
that's why he is swaying in the breeze,
still aswinging from the welcome notion.

Die Brille

Korf liest gerne schnell und viel;
darum widert ihn das Spiel
all des zwölfmal unerbetnen
Ausgewalzten, Breitgetretnen.

Meistes ist in sechs bis acht
Wörten völlig abgemacht,
und in ebensoviel Sätzen
läßt sich Bandwurmweisheit schwätzen.

Es erfindet drum sein Geist
etwas, was ihn dem entreißt:
Brillen, deren Energien
ihm den Text—zusammenziehn!

Beispielsweise dies Gedicht
läse, so bebrillt, man—nicht!
Dreiunddreißig seinesgleichen
gäben erst—Ein—Fragezeichen!!

The Spectacles

Korf reads avidly and fast.
Therefore he detests the vast
bombast of the repetitious,
twelvefold needless, injudicious.

Most affairs are settled straight
just in seven words or eight;
in as many tapeworm phrases
one can prattle on like blazes.

Hence he lets his mind invent
a corrective instrument:
Spectacles whose focal strength
shortens texts of any length.

Thus, a poem such as this,
so beglassed one would just—miss.
Thirty-three of them will spark
nothing but one question mark.

Der Träumer

Palmström stellt ein Bündel Kerzen
auf des Nachttischs Marmorplatte
und verfolgt es beim Zerschmelzen.

Seltsam formt es ein Gebirge
aus herabgeflossner Lava,
bildet Zotteln, Zungen, Schnecken.

Schwankend über dem Gerinne
stehn die Dochte mit den Flammen
gleichwie goldene Zypressen.

Auf den weißen Märchenfelsen
schaut des Träumers Auge Scharen
unverzagter Sonnenpilger.

The Dreamer

Palmstroem lights a bunch of candles
on the stone plate of his nightstand
and observes it gently melting.

Strangely, now it forms a mountain
out of downward-flowing lava,
models fringes, frostings, spirals.

Quivering above the runlets
stand the wicks with flames uprising
like a golden cypress forest.

On the white romantic rock crags
sees the dreamer's vision flocks of
dauntless sunward-striving pilgrims.

Das Polizeipferd

Palmström führt ein Polizeipferd vor.
Dieses wackelt mehrmals mit dem Ohr
und berechnet den ertappten Tropf
logarythmisch und auf Spitz und Knopf.

Niemand wagt von nun an einen Streich:
denn der Gaul berechnet ihn sogleich.
Offensichtlich wächst im ganzen Land
menschliche Gesittung und Verstand.

The Police Horse

Palm exhibits a police horse here.
This just wiggles slightly with its ear
and resolves then in the shortest time
logarithmically every crime.

No one ventures now a wicked deed
for that horse computes the same with speed.
Clearly, people everywhere get wise
and morality is on the rise.

Muhme Kunkel

Palma Kunkel ist mit Palm verwandt,
doch im Übrigen sonst nicht bekannt.
Und sie wünscht auch nicht bekannt zu sein,
lebt am liebsten ganz für sich allein.

Über Muhme Palma Kunkel drum
bleibt auch der Chronist vollkommen stumm.
Nur wo selbst sie aus dem Dunkel tritt,
teilt er dies ihr Treten treulich mit.

Doch sie trat bis jetzt noch nicht ans Licht,
und sie will es auch in Zukunft nicht.
Schon, daß hier ihr Name lautbar ward,
widerspricht vollkommen ihrer Art.

Cousin Kunkel

Palma Kunkel is a Palmstroem kin,
otherwise of unknown origin.
Nor is she desirous to be known,
and she much prefers to live alone.

Cousin Kunkel's chronicler therefore
says about her record nothing more.
Only when she leaves her privacy
on her own, he notes it faithfully.

Up to now, though, she has shunned the light
and will henceforth, too, stay out of sight.
Even that these lines her name contain
goes decidedly against her grain.

Exlibris

Ein Anonymus aus Tibris
sendet Palman ein Exlibris.

Auf demselben sieht man nichts
als den weißen Schein des Lichts.

Nicht ein Strichlein ist vorhanden.
Palma fühlt sich warm verstanden.

Und sie klebt die Blättlein rein
allenthalben dankbar ein.

Ex Libris for Palma Kunkel

An Anonymus from Tibris
sent to Palma some ex libris,

which show nothing but the bright
radiance of shining light—

nothing further. She feels good
and profoundly understood.

Grateful Palma, nice and neat,
pastes in every book a sheet.

Der Papagei

Palma Kunkels Papagei
spekuliert nicht auf Applaus;
niemals, was auch immer sei,
spricht er seine Wörter aus.

Deren Zahl ist ohne Zahl:
Denn er ist das klügste Tier,
das man je zum Kauf empfahl,
und der Zucht vollkommne Zier.

Doch indem er streng dich mißt,
scheint sein Zungenglied verdorrt.
Gleichviel, wer du immer bist,
er verrät dir nicht ein Wort.

The Parakeet

Palma Kunkel's parakeet
is no glory-seeking bird;
he stays silently discreet,
and his words are never heard.

Countless is their count; for he
is the smartest bird indeed
ever offered for a fee;
and a credit to his breed.

Sternly he will measure you,
but his tongue seems in decay;
and, no matter what you do,
not one word he'll ever say.

CARNIVAL

Die Luft

Die Luft war einst dem Sterben nah.

"Hilf mir, mein himmlischer Papa",
so rief sie mit sehr trübem Blick,
"ich werde dumm, ich werde dick;
du weisst ja sonst für alles Rat—
schick mich auf Reisen, in ein Bad,
auch saure Milch wird gern empfohlen;—
wenn nicht—laß ich den Teufel holen!"

Der Herr, sich scheuend vor Blamage,
erfand für sie die—Tonmassage.

Es gibt seitdem die Welt, die—schreit.
Wobei die Luft famos gedeiht.

The Air

The air was once about to die.

It cried: "O help me, Lord on high;
I am distressed and feeling sick,
am getting sluggish, getting thick;
you always know a way, Papa:
send me abroad, or to a spa,
or buttermilk may cure and heal—
else to the devil I'll appeal!"

The Lord, perturbed by this affair,
invented "sound massage for air."

Since then the world is full of noise,
which thrivingly the air enjoys.

Der Aesthet

Wenn ich sitze, will ich nicht
sitzen, wie mein Sitz-Fleisch möchte,
sondern wie mein Sitz-Geist sich,
säße er, den Stuhl sich flöchte.

Der jedoch bedarf nicht viel,
schätzt am Stuhl allein den Stil,
überläßt den Zweck des Möbels
ohne Grimm der Gier des Pöbels.

The Aesthete

When I sit, I do not care
just to sit to suit my hindside:
I prefer the way my mind-side
would, to sit in, build a chair.

For the mind spurns comfort, while
prizing in a stool but style;
leaves the seat's pragmatic job
gladly to the greedy mob.

Der Glaube

Eines Tags bei Kohlhaasficht
sah man etwas Wunderbares.
Doch daß zweifellos und wahr es,
dafür bürgt das Augenlicht.

Nämlich, standen dort zwei Hügel,
höchst solid und wohl bestellt;
einen schmückten Windmühlflügel
und den andern ein Kornfeld.

Plötzlich, eines Tags um viere
wechselten die Plätze sie;
furchtbar brüllten die Dorfstiere,
und der Mensch fiel auf das Knie.

Doch der Bauer Anton Metzer,
weit berühmt als frommer Mann,
sprach: ich war der Landumsetzer,
zeigt mich nur dem Landrat an.

Niemand anders als mein Glaube
hat die Berge hier versetzt.
Daß sich keiner was erlaube:
Denn ich fühle stark mich jetzt.

Aller Auge stand gigantisch
offen, als er dies erzählt.
Doch das Land war protestantisch
und in Dalldorf starb ein Held.

Faith

One fine day near Abecee
lo! a myst'ry came about.
It was true without a doubt,
as was plain for all to see.

There two hills were situated,
solid, stable, not to yield—
one was windmill-decorated,
one embellished by a field.

On that day, then, close to seven,
both changed places suddenly;
ghastly roared the bulls to heaven,
every man dropped on his knee.

But Al Metzer, local granger,
well-known pious man of peace,
said: "*I* was the landscape changer.
Go, complain to the police!

Nothing but my firm conviction
and my faith moved mountains here.
I heed no one's contradiction,
I feel strong, let this be clear!"

But this magical solution
the agnostic state denied;
sent him to an institution,
where the man, a martyr, died.

(wie jener mörderisch bezweckt)
als Strichpunkt das Gefild bedeckt! . . .

Stumm trägt man auf den Totengarten
die Semikolons beider Arten.

Was übrig von Gedankenstrichen,
kommt schwarz und schweigsam nachgeschlichen.

Das Ausrufszeichen hält die Predigt;
das Kolon dient ihm als Adjunkt.

Dann, jeder Kommaform entledigt,
stapft heimwärts man, Strich, Punkt, Strich,
Punkt . . .

(the dashes' minds are murder-bound!)
as semicolons hit the ground.

Both semicolon types they carry
in silence to the cemetarry.

The dashes who survived the war
slink after in the mourning corps.

With colon's aid, the exclamation
mark loudly mourns the victims' lot.

Then, free from comma-like formation,
they all stamp home, dash, dot, dash, dot . . .

Das Lied vom blonden Korken

Ein blonder Korke spiegelt sich
in einem Lacktablett—
allein er säh' sich dennoch nich,
selbst wenn er Augen hätt'!

Das macht, dieweil er senkrecht steigt
zu seinem Spiegelbild!
Wenn man ihn freilich seitwärts neigt,
zerfällt, was oben gilt.

O Mensch, gesetzt, du spiegelst dich
im, sagen wir,—im All!
Und senkrecht!—wärest du dann nich
ganz in demselben Fall?

The Song of the Yellow Cork

A golden cork is, mirror-wise,
shown by a polished shelf;
yet, even if endowed with eyes,
it could not see itself.

This is because it stands aligned
with its reflected view;
but if it sideways is inclined,
such is no longer true.

O man, suppose you did reflect
straight up, let's say, in space:
Would this not have the same effect
as in the stated case?

K.F.R.

Das Perfekt und das Imperfekt
    tranken Sekt.
Sie stießen aufs Futurum an
(was man wohl gelten lassen kann).

Plusquamper und Exaktfutur
    blinzten nur.

Among Tenses
[AN APPROACH]

Perfect and Past
drank to a friendship to last.
They toasted the Future tense
(which makes sense).

Futureperf and Plu
nodded too.

Der Traum der Magd

Am Morgen spricht die Magd ganz wild:
Ich hab heut nacht ein Kind gestillt—

ein Kind mit einem Käs als Kopf—
und einem Horn am Hinterschopf!

Das Horn, o denkt euch, war aus Salz
und ging zu essen, und dann—

                        "Halt's—
halt's Maul!" so spricht die Frau, "und geh
an deinen Dienst, Zä-zi-li-ē!"

The Maid's Dream

When morning came, the maid went wild
and raved: "Last night I nursed a child—

"a child who wore a cheese as head,
and from its hair a horn outspread.

"The horn—just think!—was salty, but
was fit to eat, and after . . ."

                    "Shut—
shut up," the mistress said, "and see
about your duties, Ce-ci-lee!"

I

Das Erste, des Zäzilie beflissen,
ist dies: sie nimmt von Tisch und Stuhl die Bücher
und legt sie Stück auf Stück, wie Taschentücher,
jeweils nach bestem Wissen und Gewissen.

Desgleichen ordnet sie die Schreibereien,
die Hefte, Mappen, Bleis und Gänsekiele,
vor Augen nur das eine Ziel der Ziele,
dem Genius Ordnung das Gemach zu weihen.

Denn Sauberkeit ist zwar nicht ihre Stärke,
doch Ordnung, Ordnung ist ihr eingeboren.
Ein Scheuerweib ist nicht an ihr verloren.
Dafür ist Symmetrie in ihrem Werke.

Cecily

I

For Cecily, the first concern and bother
is this: She takes the book from chairs and table
and stacks them up, as best as she is able,
like handkerchiefs each one atop the other.

She likewise tidies up, as careful warder,
the notebooks, folders, writing pens, and pencils;
she sees as goal of goals for these utensils
a room devoted to the god of order.

For cleanliness was not her strong point ever,
but order, order is her great ambition.
A cleaningwoman's job is not her mission,
but symmetry prevails in her endeavor.

II

Zäzilie soll die Fenster putzen,
sich selbst zum Gram, jedoch dem Haus zum Nutzen.

Durch meine Fenster, muß man, spricht die Frau,
so durchsehn können, dass man nicht genau
erkennen kann, ob dieser Fenster Glas
Glas oder bloße Luft ist. Merk dir das.

Zäzilie ringt mit allen Menschen-Waffen . . .
doch Ähnlichkeit mit Luft ist nicht zu schaffen.
Zuletzt ermannt sie sich mit einem Schrei—
und schlägt die Fenster allesamt entzwei!
Dann säubert sie die Rahmen von den Resten,
und ohne Zweifel ist es so am besten.
Sogar die Dame spricht zunächst verdutzt:
"So hat Zäzilie ja noch nie geputzt."

Doch alsobald ersieht man, was geschehn,
und sagt einstimmig: Diese Magd muss gehn.

II

Maid Cecily must wash the window glass;
which benefits the house, but grieves the lass.

"My windows," says Madame, "must look so well,
that no one should be able quite to tell
with full assurance whether what he sees
is glass or simply air; now mind this, please!"

Though Cecily tries all of man's devices—
to make glass look like air not one suffices.
At last she gets up nerve, and with a shout
knocks all the blasted window glasses out.
Then picks remaining splinters from the frame,
and this, without a doubt, serves best her aim.
Madame herself, perplexed at first, says, flat:
"Why, Cecily has never cleaned like that!"

But soon it is found out why this is so,
and everybody says: "This maid must go."

Die weggeworfene Flinte

Palmström findet eines Abends,
als er zwischen hohem Korn
singend schweift,
eine Flinte.

Trauernd bricht er seinen Hymnus
ab und setzt sich in den Mohn,
seinen Fund
zu betrachten.

Innig stellt er den Verzagten,
der ins Korn sie warf, sich vor
und beklagt
ihn von Herzen.

Mohn und Ähren und Cyanen
windet seine Hand derweil
still um Lauf,
Hahn und Kolben . . .

Und er lehnt den so bekränzten
Stutzen an den Kreuzwegstein,
hoffend zart,
dass der Zage,

nocheinmal des Weges kommend,
ihn erblicken möge—und—
(. . Seht den Mond
groß im Osten . .)

Oats in the Wheat Field
[AN APPROACH]

Palmstroem wandering one evening,
singing, in a field of wheat
growing tall,
finds wild oats.

Mournfully he stops his chanting
and he settles twixt the stalks
to inspect
what he found.

With compassion he imagines
him who once in dissipation
foolishly
has sown them.

And he braids of grain and poppies,
bachelor buttons, and some oats
quietly
a garland.

Then he wraps this wreath of flowers
round a mile stone, entertaining
tender hopes
that the wicked

who had sown the oats may see it
if again he passes by,
and may have
a change of heart.

Vom Zeitunglesen

Korf trifft oft Bekannte, die voll von Sorgen
wegen der sogenannten Völkerhändel. Er rät:
Lesen Sie doch die Zeitung von übermorgen.

Wenn die Diplomaten im Frühling raufen,
nimmt man einfach ein Blatt vom Herbst zur Hand
und ersieht daraus, wie alles abgelaufen.

Freilich pflegt man es umgekehrt zu machen,
und wo käme die "Jetztzeit" denn sonst auch hin!
Doch de facto sind das nur Usus-Sachen.

Reading Newspapers

Sometimes Korf meets worried friends who've read
news on international relations. He advises:
Read the paper of a day ahead!

When the diplomats start fighting in the spring
just pick up an autumn paper and
see there how they settled everything.

Mostly this is done the other way around
(else, where would it leave the present day?)
But this merely means we're habit-bound.

Die Schuhe

Man sieht sehr häufig unrecht tun,
doch selten öfter als den Schuhn.

Man weiß, daß sie nach ewgen Normen
Die Form der Füße treu umformen.

Die Sohlen scheinen auszuschweifen,
bis sie am Ballen sich begreifen.

Ein jeder merkt: es ist ein Paar.
Nur Mägden wird dies niemals klar.

Sie setzen Stiefel (wo auch immer)
einander abgekehrt vors Zimmer.

Was müssen solche Schuhe leiden!
Sie sind so fleißig, so bescheiden;

sie wollen nichts auf dieser Welt,
als daß man sie zusammenstellt,

nicht auseinanderstrebend wie
das unvernünftig blöde Vieh!

O Ihr Marie, Sophie, Therese,—
der Satan wird euch einst, der böse,

die Stiefel anziehn, wenn es heißt,
hinweg zu gehn als seliger Geist!

The Shoes

Injustice done is rarely news,
but least of all when done to shoes.

They, in accord with ancient laws,
are built to sheathe your nether paws.

The soles seem briefly to diverge
until they, at the instep, merge;

quite obviously they are a pair—
but servant maids don't seem to care:

they place the shoes, wher-e'er you go,
not face to face, but dos-à-dos.

What must those suffering shoes endure!
They are so eager, yet demure,

having one single earthly pride:
to be placed neatly side by side,

not pulling west and pulling east,
like some benighted stupid beast.

O you, Therese, Sophie, Marie,
the devil will put boots on thee

the day the death knell for you tolls
and separates you from your souls.

Dann werdet ihr voll Wehgeheule,
das Schicksal teilen jener Eule,

die, als zwei Hasen nach sie flog,
und plötzlich jeder seitwärts bog,

der eine links, der andre rechts,
zerriß (im Eifer des Gefechts)!

Wie Puppen, mitten durchgesägte,
so werdet ihr alsdann, ihr Mägde,

bei Engeln halb und halb bei Teufeln
von niegestillten Tränen träufeln,

der Hölle ein willkommner Spott
und peinlich selbst dem lieben Gott.

Then you shall share, despite your howl,
the fate of that unhappy owl,

who—following two hares in chase,
which, of a sudden, changed their pace,

one turning left, the other right—
split in the fever of the flight!

Like puppets sawed in two by blades,
you shall, thereafter, O you maids,

shed tears in never-ending spell,
in heaven half, and half in hell,

despised and scorned by Hades' king,
to God Himself embarrassing.

Der Korbstuhl

Was ich am Tage stumm gedacht,
vertraut er eifrig an der Nacht.

Mit Knisterwort und Flüsterwort
erzählt er mein Geheimnis fort.

Dann schweigt er wieder lang und lauscht—
indes die Nacht gespenstisch rauscht.

Bis ihn der Bock von neuem stößt
und sich sein Krampf in Krachen löst.

The Wicker Chair

What secretly I thought by Day
to Night she promptly gives away.

With crackling sounds and cackling sounds
my silent notions she propounds.

Then she is quiet and sits tight,
while muffled rustlings stir the Night.

Until another fit is due
and she starts chattering anew.

Tapetenblume

"Tapetenblume bin ich fein,
kehr' wieder ohne Ende,
doch statt in Mai'n und Mondenschein,
auf jeder der vier Wände.

Du siehst mich nimmerdar genung,
so weit du blickst im Stübchen,
und folgst du mir per Rösselsprung—
wirst du verrückt, mein Liebchen."

The Wallpaper Flower

"Wallpaper flower, that is I,
in May I do not bloom;
but endlessly I multiply
throughout the four-walled room.

Your eyes that search unceasingly
look for the end in vain;
and if they hopscotch after me,
my love, you go insane."

Ukas

Durch Anschlag mach ich euch bekannt:
Heut ist kein Fest im deutschen Land.
Drum sei der Tag für alle Zeit
zum Nichtfest-Feiertag geweiht.

Ukase

I make it known by proclamation:
Today's no feast day in this nation.
Wherefore this day forever may
be fêted as Nonholiday.

Der kulturbefördernde Füll

Ein wünschbar bürgerlich Idyll
erschafft, wenn du ihn trägst, der Füll.

Er kehrt, nach Vorschrift aufgehoben,
die goldne Spitze stets nach oben.

Wärst du ein Tier und sprängst auf Vieren,
er würde seinen Saft verlieren.

Trag einen Füll drum! (Du verstehst:
Damit du immer aufrecht gehst.)

The Culture-inspiring Pen

You are a cultured citizen
when carrying a fountain pen.

If you will wear it as you're told,
then UP will point the nib of gold.

Were you a beast and chased about
on fours, its juice would soon run out.

Hence wear a pen! (For then, you see,
your walk will always upright be.)

Böhmischer Jahrmarkt

I

Ein Fernrohr wird gezeigt, womit
man seinen eignen Rücken sieht.

Es führt durchs Weltall deinen Blick
im Kreis zurück auf dein Genick.

Zwar braucht es so geraume Frist,
daß du schon längst verstorben bist,

doch wird ein Standbild dir geweiht,
empfängt es ihn zu seiner Zeit.

II

Da jedermann nicht vergewärtigt,
daß man ein Standbild ihm erstellt,
wird nebenan im nächsten Zelt
ein solches Standbild angefertigt.
Drum fast ein Tor, wer nicht bestellte
daselbst für billige Gebühr
sein Monument. Den Platz dafür
vermittelt man in dritten Zelte.

III

Karten, ungeheure Karten
hängen an der Wand und warten.

Bohemian Carnival

I

The telescope that's shown in here
permits you to observe your rear:

Your gaze starts here its cosmic trek,
curves back and hits you in the neck.

There will, of course, be such delay,
you will long since have passed away;

but then, a statue in your stead
will catch that gaze when you are dead.

II

To offer everyone some aid
to buy the useful monument,
they have set up a second tent
where all these monuments are made.
He'd be a fool who would not place
his order for a bargain fee.
A realtor—tent number three—
will then provide the proper space.

III

Maps, enormous, large, and tall
hang a-waiting on the wall.

Überall in allen Ländern
stecken Stecknadeln mit Bändern.

Auf den Bändern stehn die Namen
der geehrten Herrn und Damen,

die für solche Monumente
gegen Zahlung einer Rente

dementsprechende Parzellen
freundlich zur Verfügung stellen.

Ohne jegliche Methoden
kommt man so zu Grund und Boden

sei's in Schwaben, sei's in Schweden
(von dem Nachruhm nicht zu reden).

IV

Der Summe dieser Grundstückpachter
entwächst von selbst und obendrein,
gleichsam als Interessenwächter
ein diesbezüglicher Verein.

Der Jahresbeitrag ist gebührlich,
zumal das Jahrbuch gänzlich frei,
und wer kein Sonderling natürlich
bestellt darin sein Konterfei.

Man sieht ihn dann an Ort und Stelle
mit einem Fernrohr stehn und schaun:
In Wahrheit eine Freudenquelle
für gleichgesinnte Herrn und Fraun.

Places there are pierced by jabs
where small pins display their tabs—

markers that present the names
of all gentlemen and dames

who, on payment of a rent,
will allow your monument

to be placed upon a spot
earmarked specially for your plot.

Minus trouble or debate
you acquire some real estate

In Siberia or Liberia
(not to mention fame posterior).

IV

Out of the number of lessees
in all their wide variety
will spring as—shall we say—trustees
an apposite society.

The yearly dues are not too high,
a yearbook is included free,
and everyone, save cranks, will buy
some space in it as portraitee.

He will appear then in location,
his pupil fastened to the glass,
indeed a source of inspiration
for each likeminded lad and lass.

V

Doch wie gesagt, trotz allem Streben
läßt der ertrachtete Effekt
sich nicht persönlich mehr erleben.

Die weitre Regelung bezweckt
die Herme. Nebenbei indessen
darf man sich selbst nicht ganz vergessen.

Man stirbt, wenn auch nicht heut und morgen.
Und will man dann begraben sein,
so muß man doch auch dafür sorgen.

Und dies tut wieder ein Verein,
und zwar begräbt er wie die Norm
im Sockel Sie und Aschenform.

VI

Dies alles und noch mehr ist Ihnen
vielleicht ein wenig viel erschienen.
Jedoch von Ihrer Ruhe trennt
Sie schließlich nichts als ein—Agent.

Ein Stellvertreter, dem Sie jährlich
ein Fixum zahlen, nicht zu spärlich,
wird Ihnen gegen ein Entgelt
im Nebenzimmer vorgestellt . . .

V

However anxious you may be—
as we have mentioned: the effect
you will not likely live to see.

The further plan is with respect
to stelae. Also, in addition,
do not forget you own condition:

You, too, will die (though there's no hurry),
yet funeral propriety
need cause you not the slightest worry:

a similar society
will do the chore and seemly burn
your corpse and place it in an urn.

VI

All this commotion seems to you
perhaps a bit too much ado;
an agent, though, may be assigned
to let you keep your peace of mind.

And in the tent next door you can
be introduced to such a man.
(They charge for it: This deputy
is paid a lump-sum annual fee.)

Wir hoffen, daß Sie sich ihn mieten.
Sie finden wahrlich nirgends nichts
so Vorteilhaftes angesichts
des Ungeheuren, das wir bieten:

Ein Fernrohr, schlechterdings ein Wunder,
ein Grab, ein Denkmal, ein Stück Grund
befreit Sie von dem ganzen Plunder.
Wo nicht, erscheint ein Stehmann und—

Sie zaudern noch! Wir geben glatt
das erste Schaltjahr in Rabatt.

We hope you'll hire one of those.
You surely won't find anywhere
a bargain buy that can compare.
Consider, please, what we propose:

A telescope, indeed inspiring,
a statue, tombstone, plot of land,
and—if you feel this is too tiring—
an agent who takes over and . . .

You hesitate? Well, let us see—
we'll throw one leap year in for free!

ACKNOWLEDGMENTS

The publication of this volume, which has been in the making for a long time, will be greeted with relief by my friends and colleagues in the Editorial Department of the University of California Press whom I used as guinea pigs for individual lines or words and who were indulgent with my hobby: Lucie, Glenn, Miriam, Joel, John—in fact, all of them at one time or another. My good breadgiver August surprised me with detailed and welcome suggestions.

My life-long pen brother Joe Fabry, with whom I have been sharing the nom de guerre of Peter Fabrizius since our student days, this time lets me gather the glory and the blame for the present effort myself, although he was a patient and helpful godfather as each new verse child was born.

My special thanks go to resourceful Karl F. Ross of New York who went over the translations with a sharp eye and a fine word sense making many excellent improvements; in the process he caught fire himself and generously contributed some translations of his own: Raven Ralph, Seagulls, Hawken Chick, Yellow Cork, and the first six of the Fairyland section. Palmstroem is a joint effort, and the Funnels are a double effort—one his and one mine; I could not decide which to choose, and so I included both, mercifully unidentified. The assonances in Naturspiel and Träumer I ignored in the translation, over his objection.

Professor B. Q. Morgan of Stanford added some appreciated final touches when the manuscript was in proof.

Permission to print the original German poems was given by Insel-Verlag, Frankfurt am Main.

The line-drawing vignettes are doodles by Christian Morgenstern himself.

Berkeley, California   M.E.K.
January, 1963

227